The Tree

John Dunstall fecit.

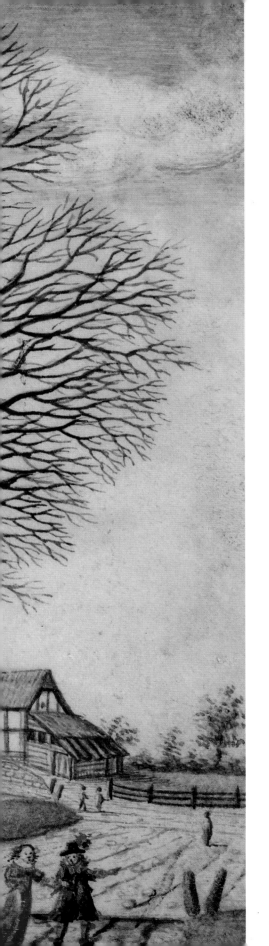

The Tree
Meaning and Myth

Frances Carey

THE BRITISH MUSEUM PRESS

*To my colleagues at the British Museum and
Royal Botanic Gardens Kew, from whom I have
learnt so much*

© 2012 The Trustees of the British Museum

Frances Carey has asserted the right to be identified as the author of this work

First published in 2012 by The British Museum Press
A division of The British Museum Company Ltd
38 Russell Square, London WC1B 3QQ

britishmuseum.org/publishing

A catalogue record for this book is available from the British Library

ISBN: 978-0-7141-5085-7

Designed by Raymonde Watkins

Printed in China by 1010 Printing International Ltd

The vast majority of the objects illustrated in this book are in the collection of
the British Museum. Their Museum registration numbers and donor information
are given on pp. 187–8. You can find out more about objects in all areas of the
British Museum's collection on the Museum's website at britishmuseum.org/
research/search_the_collection_database.aspx

Half-title page Nicholas Hilliard (*c.* 1547–*c.* 1619), reverse of the 'Dangers
averted' medal celebrating the defeat of the Spanish Armada. *c.* 1589
(see p. 115)
Frontispiece John Dunstall (d. 1693), A pollard oak near West Hampnett Place,
Chichester. *c.* 1660 (see p. 154)
'An Arboretum', page 60 Walter Crane (1845–1915), Orchard scene (detail).
1874. Watercolour and bodycolour, 22.9 x 31.8 cm.

CONTENTS

டைடகெண்டைத்தொடிபட்டுணாமதேஸ்தமணிசணடைசெ
தணடபணிமணிகுமேலேவசெத்தமிடேமணடேகோலலிதாரம்
தீபபேளாயிடம்

மடுமிமதனனதொவணனபதினாலாபடிம இலணகில்
மமணுகுமுதணடையாணிடம்

INTRODUCTION

Once upon a time trees were temples of the deities, and in conformity with primitive ritual simple country places even now dedicate a tree of exceptional height to a god; nor do we pay greater worship to images shining with gold and ivory than to the forests and to the very silences that they contain. The different kinds of trees are kept perpetually dedicated to their own divinities, for instance, the chestnut-oak to Jove, the bay to Apollo, the olive to Minerva, the myrtle to Venus, the poplar to Hercules.

Pliny the Elder, *Natural History*, Book XII (AD 77–9)[1]

A well-kempt forest begs Our Lady's grace;
Someone is not disgusted, or at least
Is laying bets upon the human race
Retaining enough decency to last;
The trees encountered on a country stroll
Reveal a lot about a country's soul.

W.H. Auden, *Bucolics, II: Woods* (for Nicolas Nabokov) (1979)[2]

TREES HAVE ALWAYS been at the heart of mankind's relationship to the natural and the supernatural worlds, a relationship that serves as an index of both ecological and spiritual well-being. Nowhere has the imaginative power of trees and of the memory attributed to them been more evident than in relation to sacred groves or the 'forests and . . . the very silences that they contain'. In ancient Mesopotamia (modern Iraq), the cedar forest appeared as the realm of the gods in the epic of Gilgamesh, the world's oldest work of literature, composed some four to five thousand years ago. Gilgamesh slays Humbaba, the monster appointed to guard the forest, indiscriminately felling trees in his triumph; the epic thus recognized the symbolic significance of the forest and mankind's reckless disregard for nature, with all that this entails.

Another ancient poem, Virgil's *Aeneid* of the first century BC, was equally in thrall to the magical powers of the forest. It related the founding legend of Rome in which the prince Aeneas, fleeing after the fall of Troy, arrives at Avernus on the coast west of Naples, which was believed to be the gateway to the underworld. There he is guided to the golden bough that alone can grant him passage to the place where he shall gaze on 'the Forests of Styx, the land which is pathless to the living'.[3] The golden bough is often identified as European mistletoe, *Viscum album* (see fig. 6), a parasite that grows on a variety

Cotton textile (detail) depicting the Forest Sequence (Aranya Kanda) from the Ramayana (see fig. 1).

of host trees including the oak, sacred to the god Zeus/Jupiter/Jove. Travelling up the Tiber Aeneas comes to the site of Rome's future glory, where the woods 'used to be the home of native Fauns and Nymphs, and a race of men who were born from tree-trunks of tough wood'.[4]

The forest is important to the narrative of a third great epic, this time from South Asia, the Ramayana, whose core texts mostly date from the fifth or fourth century BC (fig. 1). Rama the hero, robbed of the crown to his kingdom of Ayodyha, lives for thirteen years in exile with his wife Sita and brother Lakshmana in the forest of Dandaka, the largest of all the ancient forests of India. In southern Nigeria sacred groves are significant to the Edo and Yoruba people as places of worship for deities such as the white-faced Olokun, who rules the sea. The first of the brass crowned heads from the medieval kingdom of Ife was discovered in such a setting in 1910. This head, and others found in the city of Ife itself in 1938, would have been displayed in groves on ceremonial occasions as part of the ancestor cult of the kingdom's rulers (fig. 2).

1 ABOVE Cotton textile (detail) depicting the Forest Sequence from the Ramayana. Made in Tamil Nadu, southern India, or Sri Lanka, 19th century. 103 x 755 cm (whole).

2 LEFT Cast brass head of an Oni (ruler). Yoruba people, Ife, Nigeria, 12th–15th century. H. 36 cm.

THE ANTIQUITY OF TREES

The real origins of trees far exceed even the most extravagant legendary claims for their antiquity. Study of the fossil evidence has established that the first appearance of land plants occurred about 410 million years ago. Some forty to fifty million years afterwards came organisms whose water-conducting tubes were lignified or woody, thus producing the structure that helps to define what are considered to be 'trees' (fig. 3). By contrast the first primates did not appear until sixty million years ago, and the first hominids at most five to six million years ago.

Trees regarded as intrinsic to the history of the British Isles, such as oak, alder and hazel, have waxed and waned according to the fluctuations in climate over the last two million years (fig. 4). That is a mere sliver of time compared with the history of another island, the biodiversity 'hotspot' of Madagascar, home to a variety of animal and plant species that are only found in that location. Trees that have evolved there over millions of years in isolation include six of the eight species of *Adansonia*, the baobab tree, which are only found on Madagascar, with a seventh that also grows on the African mainland (see p. 62).

Among the ancient living wonders of the arboreal world are the so-called 'Methusalehs' such as the Fortingall Yew by Loch Tay in Scotland, supposedly the oldest tree in Europe at more than 2000 years old. This is outstripped, though, by the remarkable bristlecone pines of the White Mountains in eastern California, some of which are approaching 5000 years of age.

TREES AND THE BRITISH MUSEUM

Trees have been at the root of the British Museum since it was created in 1753 through the bequest of one of the greatest of all natural history collectors, Sir Hans Sloane (1660–1753). Sloane's herbarium or collection of dried plants, mounted on album sheets, and his

3 TOP RIGHT *Archaeopteris hibernica*, foliage preserved in yellow sandstone from the earliest tree progymnosperms (extinct group of 'woody' spore-bearing plants). From Kilkenny, Ireland. L. 25 cm. (Natural History Museum, London).

4 RIGHT The Sweet Track (detail), a raised plankway that ran across a reed swamp in the Somerset levels, near Glastonbury, England. It was made of oak, ash and lime, with rails and pegs mainly of hazel and alder. Tree-ring evidence shows it was built in 3807/6 BC. The track is named after Ray Sweet, who found it during peat excavations in 1970.

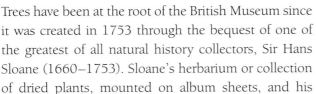

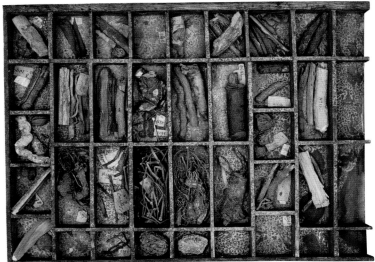

5 Volumes from Sir Hans Sloane's herbarium and a tray of his 'vegetable substances'. (Natural History Museum, London. A selection is on loan to the Enlightenment Gallery in the British Museum).

trays of 'vegetable substances' – seeds, fruit, bark, roots and gums (fig. 5) – included large numbers of specimens brought together from pioneering expeditions around the world. One of these was his own voyage to Jamaica in 1687–9, where he identified as many as eight hundred new species.[5] Another outstanding figure of botanical significance in the early history of the British Museum was Sir Joseph Banks (1743–1820), who was a Trustee of the Museum and the unofficial director of the Royal Botanic Gardens at Kew. One of the first employees of the British Museum was a pupil of the Swedish botanist Linnaeus, Daniel Solander (1733–82), whose task from 1763 was to begin sorting Sloane's collection. Five years later Solander faced his greatest challenge when he accompanied Joseph Banks on the first of Captain Cook's voyages to the South Seas (1768–71). Moored at what is now Sydney, New South Wales, Cook wrote in his log for 6 May 1770: 'The great quantity of New Plants that Mr Banks and Dr Solander collected in this place occasioned my giving it the name of Botany Bay.'[6]

Eventually the natural history collections outgrew the capacity of the British Museum's building in Bloomsbury and departed for South Kensington, where the Natural History Museum opened in 1881. But traces of these botanical interests remain at the British Museum, especially in the albums of drawings and watercolours from Sloane's bequest, and in treasures that arrived later on, such as the 'paper mosaics' of Mary Delany. She made nearly a thousand of these in the 1770s in imitation of a 'hortus siccus' or 'garden' of dried flowers (fig. 6), drawing upon plants at the Chelsea Physic Garden, many supplied by Sir Joseph Banks from the Queen's garden at Kew, and the botanical collections put together by the Duchess of Portland and other friends:

So now DELANY forms her mimic bowers,
Her paper foliage, and her silken flowers;
Her virgin train the tender scissors ply,
Vein the green leaf, the purple petal dye . . .

Erasmus Darwin, *The Loves of Plants* (1789)[7]

Such works of record and of art were properly part of a collection dedicated to the history of the world as told through man-made objects, which was the British Museum's focus from the 1880s onwards. It is through these artefacts that the subject of trees is approached in this book as part of a broad cultural history which embraces science and art, travel and trade, poetry and prose, mythology, belief and ritual. The book begins by looking at the development of our knowledge of trees – their identification and cultivation – then explores the impact made by voyages of discovery and the fascination with 'deep time' in the nineteenth century. Advances in geological knowledge, combined with Charles Darwin's evolutionary theories, changed the whole understanding of what really constituted the 'tree of life':

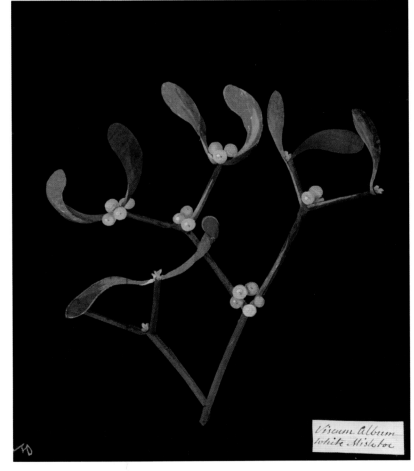

6 Mary Delany (1700–1788), *Viscum album*, white mistletoe. 1776. Collage of coloured papers with bodycolour and watercolour on a black ink background, 28.4 x 21.3 cm.

As buds give rise by growth to fresh buds, and these, if vigorous, branch out and overtop on all sides many a feebler branch, so by generation I believe it has been with the great Tree of Life, which fills with its dead and broken branches the crust of the earth, and covers the surface with its ever branching and beautiful ramifications.[8]

The metaphor of the 'tree of life' is the focus of the second chapter, which introduces the significance of trees in myth, religion and art. Then follows an 'arboretum', profiling twenty-five trees, arranged alphabetically according to the Latin name for each genus, followed by its English common name. Finally, the epilogue returns to the opening quotation by W.H. Auden to review mankind's treatment of trees and assess what bets have been laid upon the human race.

11

CHAPTER ONE

THE KNOWLEDGE OF TREES

THE KNOWLEDGE OF TREES

'WHAT'S IN A NAME?'

'A great deal' is the short answer to the question posed by Shakespeare's Juliet, which is often used to introduce the principles of classification.[1] 'That which we call a rose/By any other name would smell as sweet',[2] but names alone, without an agreed basis for the identification, quickly become meaningless. In the West, the systematization of the botanical world is heavily indebted to the scholarship of ancient Greece, particularly the work of Theophrastus (*c.* 371–287 BC). He was a pupil of Aristotle, the teacher of Alexander the Great, whose campaigns in Asia in the early fourth century BC added greatly to the stock of botanical and horticultural knowledge. In the treatises *Enquiry into Plants* and *On the Causes of Plants*, Theophrastus distinguished plants as woody and herbaceous, classifying them according to their habits of growth, their localities, sizes, practical applications and economic uses.

The first drawings to accompany botanical descriptions were attributed around 75 BC to Krateuas, the personal physician of a formidable opponent of the Romans, Mithridates VI (134–63 BC), King of Pontus in northern Anatolia (now part of Turkey). According to the Roman author Pliny the Elder, in his encyclopaedic *Natural History* (AD 77–9):

> Krateuas, Dionysios and Metrodoros adapted a most attractive method, though one which makes clear little else except the difficulty of employing it. For they painted likenesses of the plants and then wrote under them their properties. But not only is a picture misleading when the colours are so many, particularly as the aim is to copy nature, but besides this, much imperfection arises from the manifold hazards in the accuracy of copyists. In addition, it is not enough for each plant to be painted at one period only of its life, since it alters its appearance with the fourfold changes of the year.[3]

The pharmacological properties of plants, rather than their economic uses, were of paramount interest well into the early modern period of the late sixteenth and seventeenth centuries. A principal source of study was *De Materia Medica*, written about AD 65 by the Greek physician Dioscorides, and translated into Latin around the sixth century. It attempted to order plants first by category or class and then according to the effect on the body, instead of presenting the material in alphabetical sequence. Another pre-eminent contribution was made by the Persian polymath known by his Latinized name Avicenna (*c.* 980–1037), who described the medicinal herbs of southern Spain, North Africa and the eastern Mediterranean.

The botanical frame of reference for Europeans expanded apace as other continents of the world revealed their riches. The strangeness and variety of the vegetation encountered by Spanish Jesuits in the Americas in the sixteenth century led them to believe that God must have created two quite different Gardens of Eden. Following hard on the heels of the Spanish came French and British voyages to the eastern seaboard of North America, where new species of plants were recorded and every effort was made to import them for cultivation. In England John Tradescant the Younger (1608–62), who succeeded his father as botanist to Charles I and Queen Henrietta Maria in 1638, introduced several of the most striking trees of the North American east coast to the garden that he and his father had created in Lambeth beside the Thames: bald cypress (*Taxodium distichum*), eastern red cedar (*Juniperus virginiana*), black locust (*Robinia pseudoacacia*) and the tulip tree (*Lirodendron tulipifera*).

With the influx of new species it became imperative to establish improved systems of classification based on first-hand empirical study. Two notable seventeenth-century figures in this connection were John Ray (1627–1705) and Nehemiah Grew (1641–1712). A naturalist and close friend of Sir Hans Sloane, John Ray travelled widely, publishing the results of his observations in *Historia Plantarum* (1686–1704). He was the first to use the word 'species' in its modern scientific sense, noting that 'no matter what variations occur in the individual or the species, if they spring from the seed of one and the same plant, they are accidental variations and not such as to distinguish a species'.[4] The physician Nehemiah Grew devoted his life to the study of the structure of plants, taking advantage of the new invention of the microscope to examine their morphology in order to ascertain 'visible communities with other plants'.[5] His methodology was detailed in a series of papers presented to the Royal Society, of which he was Secretary from 1677:

> To examine, again, not only all the *Parts*, but *Kinds of Vegetables*, and comparatively, to observe divers of the same *size*, *shape*, *motion*, *age*, *sap*, *quality*, *power*, or any other way the *same*, which may also agree, in some one or more particulars, as to their *Interior Structure*: and to make this comparison, throughout all their *Parts* and *Properties*. To observe them likewise, in several *Seasons* of the year, and in several *Ages* of the *Plants*, and of their *Parts*; in both which, divers of them may be noted to change, not only their *Dimensions*, but their *Natures* also; as *Vessels*, do into *Ligaments*; and *Cartilages*, into *Bones*, sometimes, in *Animals*. And to do all this by several Ways of *section*, Oblique, Perpendicular, and Transverse; all three being requisite, if not to Observe, yet the better to Comprehend, some Things. And it will be convenient sometimes to Break, Tear, or otherwise Divide, without a *Section*. Together with the *Knife* it will be necessary to joyn the *Microscope*; and to examine all the *Parts*, and in every Way, in the use of That.[6]

The greatest of all plant collections was that of the British Museum's founder, Sir Hans Sloane, who succeeded Sir Isaac Newton as President of the Royal Society in 1727. A physician like Grew, whose natural history specimens he acquired, Sloane's herbarium was important because of its size, scope and availability to the many visitors who came to Sloane's house, first in Bloomsbury then in Chelsea, where he lived from 1742 until his death in 1753. In 1696 Sloane published the plants he had observed on his visit to Jamaica in 1687–9.[7] His efforts were praised by John Ray, who noted that he had 'done botanists great service in distributing or reducing the confused heap of names, and contracting the number of species'.[8] The material grew apace, and when the Swedish botanist Carl Linnaeus (1707–78) visited Sloane in Bloomsbury in July 1736, he described the collection as being in 'complete disorder'. Where the plants were identified, Sloane followed John Ray's system of classification, based on the careful description of key distinguishing features of each example. However accurately observed, this approach resulted in lengthy 'phrase names' or polynomials, and frequent duplication, which began to create havoc in the horticultural trade by the second quarter of the eighteenth century, when the same plants were being sold to customers several times over under different names. The Society of Gardeners, founded in 1724 by Philip Miller of Chelsea Physic Garden and the commercial nurseryman Thomas Fairchild, attempted to provide a standardized nomenclature for 'Exotic and domestic plants propagated for Sale, In the Gardens near London' in its *Catalogus Plantarum*. But though many more drawings were made in readiness, only a single volume was ever published (in 1730), which failed to provide the standardization sought by Miller and Fairchild. The Society's efforts were the subject of ridicule in a pamphlet of 1732, *The Natural History of the Arbor Vitae, or Tree of Life*:

> The *Tree of Life* is a succulent plant, consisting of one only straight Stem, on the Top of which is a *Pistillum* or *Apex*, at some times *glandiform*, and resembling a May-Cherry, tho' at others more like the *Nut* of the *Avellana*, or *Filberd-Tree* . . . It is produced in most Countries, tho' it thrives more in some than in others . . . It chears the Heart, and exhilarates the mind, quiets Jarrs, Feuds and Discontents . . . If any Person is desirous to see this excellent and wondrous Plant in good Perfection, he may see it at the aforemention'd Mr. B--------n's Garden at *Lambeth*, who calls it the *Silver-Spoon Tree*, and is at all times ready to oblige his Friends with the Sight of it.

Linnaeus devised a method of classification based on sexual characteristics (the inspiration for the poem *The Loves of Plants*, published in 1789 by Erasmus Darwin, grandfather of Charles; see p. 11), and, most importantly, came up with a two-part or binomial naming system, which he published in *Species Plantarum* of 1753. He understood that for scientific names to be of value as identifiers, they must have a clear and

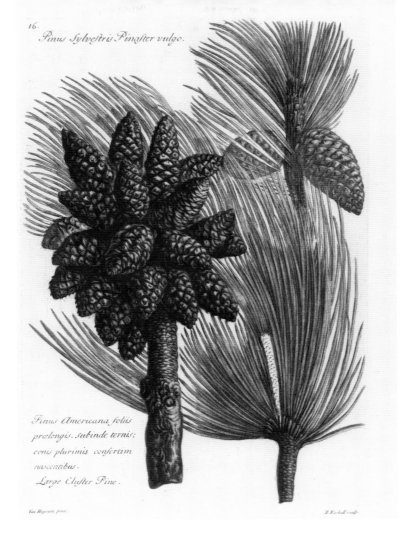

stable hierarchy. His binomials for the individual plants gave first the genus, followed by the 'trivial name', which is that of the particular species within the larger grouping. The merit of this system becomes clear by comparing for example, the Linnaean name *Pinus pinaster* (for what is commonly called the cluster, maritime or pinaster pine) with the Latin name given in the *Catalogus Plantarum* of 1730: *Pinus americana folius praelongis, subinde ternis; conis plurimus consertim nascentibus* (fig. 7).[9] Linnaeus's *Species Plantarum* remains the basis of the modern International Code of Botanical Nomenclature (ICBN), whose principle is that each plant has only one correct name within a particular classification that is accepted worldwide.

THE CULTIVATION OF TREES

The elaborate mythologies that have grown up around trees, and the romantic appeal of their physical attributes, have never precluded a pragmatic approach to their cultivation, management and sometimes ruthless exploitation. Archaeological evidence from around 7000 BC shows that tracts of woodland in parts of Europe were being cleared to encourage

7 Elisha Kirkall (*c.* 1682–1742), after Jacobus van Huysum (1687/9–1740), cluster pine (left), with *Pinus sylvestris*, Scots pine (right). Pl. 16 of the Society of Gardeners' *Catalogus Plantarum*, 1730. Colour mezzotint, 37.9 x 25.3 cm.

the growth of hazel, whose nuts provided a highly nutritious food source (fig. 8).[10] The earliest written accounts of arboriculture appear on clay tablets from Mesopotamia (modern Iraq), dating from four thousand years ago. The tablet illustrated here (fig. 9) records the cultivation of orchards, specifying areas, numbers of fruit trees (date palms, pomegranates and apples) and the names of the gardeners. Alexander the Great's campaigns eastwards across Asia transformed the arboriculture of Greece, and then other parts of Europe, introducing not only different varieties of trees, but also techniques of cultivation such as grafting (fig. 10).

In his *Essay on the Geography of Plants* (1807), the great German botanist and explorer Alexander von Humboldt (1769–1859) paid tribute to the importance of western Asia as the route by which many orchard trees came to Europe:

> South and east of the Caspian sea, on the banks of the Amu Darya, in the ancient Colchis and especially in the province of Kurdistan . . . there the land is covered with lemon trees, pomegranate trees, cherry trees, pear trees and all the fruit trees that we grow in our gardens . . . Situated between the Euphrates and the Indus, between the Caspian Sea and the Persian Gulf, these fertile lands gave Europe its most precious products. Persia gave us the walnut tree and the peach tree; Armenia, the apricot tree; Asia Minor, the cherry tree and the chestnut tree; Syria, the fig tree, the pear tree, the pomegranate tree, the olive tree, the plum tree, and the mulberry tree. In Cato's time, the Romans did not yet know the cherry, the peach, or the mulberry. Hesiod and Homer already mention the cultivation of the olive tree in Greece and in the islands of the Archipelago. In the reign of Tarquinius the Ancient, the tree did not yet exist in Italy, Spain, or Africa. During Appius Claudius's consulate, oil was very scarce in Rome; but by Pliny's time the olive tree had already spread to France and Spain.[11]

DNA analysis has shown the origins of many of the above trees to be more complex than Humboldt knew. Apples, apricots and peaches, for example, came from China and Central Asia, spreading westwards along the network of routes known as the Silk Road.

The influence of classical authors, both practical and poetic, remained a principal source of information on plant domestication throughout much of the nineteenth century. Living in the woods on Walden Pond near Concord, Massachusetts, from 1845 to 1847, the American author Henry Thoreau (1817–62) described how he would turn for advice to 'Old Cato [Cato the Censor], whose De Re Rustica [On Farming; *c.* 185 BC] is my "Cultivator"'.[12] Nowhere was poetry and farming more closely intertwined than in the writings of the Roman author

8 Hazelnut husks, found with bark inside an oak tree-trunk coffin within an Early Bronze Age (2150–1600 BC) barrow at Loose Howe, on the eastern moorlands of Yorkshire.

9 Clay tablet inscribed in cuneiform script with records of the cultivation of orchards. Third dynasty of Ur, 2100–2000 BC. H. 9.8 cm.

Virgil (70–19 BC). His *Georgics* (*c*. 29 BC) was a didactic poem in four books that extolled the husbandry essential to the fulfilment of a virtuous life. In Book II Virgil moved between invoking the divinities associated with the woodlands and with particular trees, to passages that describe in detail the propagation and growth of trees, including interventions that remain familiar the world over, such as grafting, transplanting, fertilizing with manure and pruning (figs 10–12). Pliny's *Natural History* devoted eight books to trees and the drugs derived from them, distinguishing between cultivated trees and those of the forest.

Horticulture and arboriculture soon featured in early printed books. The first manual in English dedicated to the art of gardening appeared in 1582, followed by John Manwood's treatise on Forest Laws in 1592 and William Lawson's *The New Orchard and Garden with the Country Housewife's Garden* in 1618. John Gerard's *Herball* (1597), John Parkinson's *Paradisi in Sole* (*Paradise in the Sun*, 1629) and *Theatrum Botanicum: The Theatre of Plants* (1640) all contained a wealth of information on what was being grown in London.

John Evelyn's *Sylva, or A Discourse of Forest Trees and the Propagation of Timber in his Majesties Dominions* (1664) was the first book published by the Royal Society, founded after the restoration of the monarchy under Charles II in 1660. It was written in response to the king's urgent need of timber for the navy (which became the Royal Navy in 1661).

10 Hans Weiditz (*c*. 1500–*c*. 1536), An emperor grafting a tree. 1522. Woodcut, 9.7 x 15.4 cm.

This is an illustration from *Von der Artzney bayder Glück* (Medicine against both Fortunes), the German version of Petrarch's 'Book of Fortune', *De Remediis utriusque fortunae*, a book of practical philosophy written in 1360. Weiditz worked in Augsburg during the reign of Emperor Maximilian I.

11 Edward Burne-Jones (1833–98), 'Key of Spring', from *The Flower Book*. 1882–98. Watercolour and bodycolour touched with gold, Diam. 16.9 cm.

A figure unlocks a tree so that the sap may rise.

12 Fred Williams (1927–82), Tree pruning. 1955–6. Etching and drypoint, 11.2 x 22.5 cm.

One of more than 100 etchings that the artist made in London between 1952 and 1956, before returning to Australia.

13 Ludwig Pfleger (1726–95), Studies of the flowers, trunk, cones and seeds of a larch tree (*Larix decidua*, European larch), formerly in an album dated 1788. Watercolour, 53.7 x 37.9 cm.

This sheet came from an album of sixty-nine drawings titled 'True likeness from nature of all the species of wood, such as coniferous and deciduous trees, as well as bushes, shrubs and plants, to be found in the neighbourhood of Baaden. Drawn and painted by Ludvic Pfleger, Captain in the Service of The Margrave of Baden Ao.1788.'

The perils of deforestation, so often a man-made disaster, have been cause for concern throughout recorded history, but Evelyn, a staunch Royalist, was particularly critical of the depredations to timber during the Commonwealth (1649–60). He inveighed against:

> . . . this Iron-age amongst us, who have lately made so prodigious a spoil of those goodly Forests, Woods and Trees (to satisfy an impious and unworthy Avarice). For it has not been the late increase of shipping alone, the multiplication of Glass-works, Iron-Furnaces, and the like, from whence this impolitick diminution of our Timber has proceeded; but from the disproportionate spreading of Tillage, caused through that prodigious havock made by such as . . . were tempted, not only to fell and cut down, but utterly to grub up, demolish, and raze, as it were all those many goodly Woods, and Forests, which our more prudent Ancestors left standing, for the Ornament, and service of their country.[13]

The demands of Charles II's expansion of the navy were considerable: two thousand well-grown oaks were needed to build a third-rate 74-gun warship. The British navy remained dependent on oak until 1860, when steamships built of iron were introduced.

The science of forestry was born in Germany in the latter half of the eighteenth century, when new methods of forest management were introduced, based on mass or volume of wood rather than quantity of trees and area alone. Foresters could project the growth of trees and prescribe time frames for their felling. It became ever more important to understand all parts of the tree (fig. 13), leading to the development of wood libraries or xylotheks. The first recorded example belonged to Carl Schildbach in Kassel in 1785, a 'collection of around 300 books in a glass cabinet in his living room . . . they are little wooden caskets in book form, each one containing the whole natural history of the tree and kind of wood which grows in the Landgraftschaft Hessen'.[14] Other examples of xylotheks dating from the late 1780s to 1815 can be found in Munich, Passau, Landshut, Freising and Graz. The Japanese produced a variation comprising painted wooden panels rather than actual specimens, illustrative of trees important to their country. A 'xylarium' was brought to the Rijksherbarium in Leiden around 1830; another from 1878 is among the collections at Kew.

The advances made in British horticulture were among the reasons why Linnaeus sent his pupil Daniel Solander to England in 1760. The doyen of horticulture at that time was Philip Miller, chief gardener of the Chelsea Physic Garden from 1722 until 1771 and author of the hugely influential *Gardeners' Dictionary* of 1731. This was dedicated to Sir Hans Sloane, who had purchased the manor of Chelsea in 1712, giving the freehold of the Physic Garden the following year to the Society of Apothecaries, who had leased the ground since 1673. Miller was initially resistant to Linnaean binomial nomenclature but, by the eighth edition of the *Dictionary* in 1768, he had adopted binomials. Nurseries abounded across London and its environs, catering to the demand from wealthy customers who vied with each other for the most exotic foreign imports. Peter Collinson, whose estate at Mill Hill in Middlesex was visited by Solander, could order 1000 cedars of Lebanon saplings from a butcher in Barnes who also ran a small nursery business. John Bartram in Philadelphia, who was designated the King's Botanist for North America in 1765, worked closely with Collinson and supplied boxes of seeds and cuttings to sixty subscribers over a thirty-year period in the mid-eighteenth century. Their efforts helped to transform the appearance of many private parks through the introduction of American trees with a far greater range of colour than native species. However, it was developments in the nineteenth century, most notably the work of Charles Darwin, that were to have the most far-reaching consequences for the understanding and cultivation of trees, as for all other aspects of the natural world.

WORLDS LOST AND FOUND

By the mid-nineteenth century geological, palaeontological and botanical investigation had revealed a timescale of ever-increasing depth for the earth, its vegetation and inhabitants. This posed a decisive challenge to the biblical version of the Creation calculated by James Ussher (1581–1656), Archbishop of Armagh, as having taken place on the night before 23 October 4004 BC. The Flood, given the date of 2349–8 BC, was central to this history of the earth, marking a cataclysmic rupture between an antediluvian age and the world thereafter, inhabited by the survivors from Noah's Ark and their descendants. Such was the background of religious belief to the work of Charles Darwin, and that of his mentors

and associates. Foremost among these were the geologist Charles Lyell (1797–1875) and the botanist Joseph Hooker (1817–1911), who succeeded his father William as Director at Kew in 1865. Darwin read Lyell's *Principles of Geology* (1830–33) on the voyage of HMS *Beagle* to South America in 1832–6, a trip that laid the foundation of his work on the 'mutability' of species, which eventually appeared as *On the Origin of Species by Means of Natural Selection* in 1859. The account of the voyage, published in 1830, concluded with 'A Very Few Remarks Concerning the Deluge' by Captain Robert Fitzroy, the naval officer in charge, who attempted to reconcile the scientific observations of Darwin and others with the 'true' meaning of the biblical narrative.

Crucial to expanding the botanical frame of reference were the voyages of Captain Cook and others from 1770 onwards, which disclosed the unique nature of both flora and fauna in Australia. Alexander von Humboldt and Aimé Bonpland's expedition to the Americas in 1799–1804 resulted in the description of 8000 plant species, half of which were new. Their account fired the imagination of the young Charles Darwin, along with images of lush tropical landscapes such as the Brazilian forest depicted in a lithograph of 1828 by Moritz Rugendas

14 Moritz Rugendas (1802–58), The Brazilian forest. 1828. Lithograph, 62 x 50 cm.

(fig. 14), author of *Voyage pittoresque dans le Brésil* (1827–35). An impression of the print belonged to one of Darwin's tutors at Cambridge, the botanist John Stevens Henslow, to whom Darwin wrote from Brazil in 1832: 'I first saw a Tropical Forest in all its sublime grandeur. – Nothing, but the reality can give you any idea, how wonderful, how magnificent the scene is . . . Your engraving is exactly true, but underrates, rather than exaggerates the luxuriance – I never experienced such intense delight.'[15]

Public fascination with new and exotic vistas – both geographical and chronological – was stoked by science fiction authors such as Jules Verne (1828–1905). In *Journey to the Centre of the Earth* (published in Paris in 1864, translated into English in 1871), Verne tells that:

15 George Baxter (1804–67), *The Crystal Palace and Gardens*. 1854. Colour wood-engraving, 11.2 x 15.9 cm.

After about a mile, we saw the edge of an immense forest . . . It displayed the vegetation of the Tertiary Period in all its splendour. Great palm trees of species no longer existing and superb palmaceae, pines, yews, cypress, and thujas represented the coniferous family, all joined together by an impenetrable network of creepers . . . Then there appeared, all intermixed and intertwined, trees from highly different countries on the face of the globe, the oak growing beside the palm-tree, the Australian eucalyptus leaning on the Norwegian fir, the northern birch mingling its branches with the New Zealand kauri. It was enough to upset the sanity of the most ingenious classifiers of terrestrial botany.

Suddenly I stopped short. I held my uncle back. The uniform light made it possible to see the smallest objects in the depths of the thicket. I thought I saw, no I really *did* see, enormous shapes wandering around under the trees! They were in fact gigantic animals, a whole herd of mastodons no longer fossil, but fully alive, and resembling the ones whose remains were discovered in the bogs of Ohio in 1801.

So the dream where I had seen the rebirth of this complete world from prehistoric times, combining the Tertiary and Quaternary Periods, had finally become reality! And we were there, alone, in the bowels of the Earth, at the mercy of its fierce inhabitants![16]

If Verne's characters had to descend to the nether regions to catch their glimpse of an antediluvian age, from 1854 visitors to the Crystal Palace at Sydenham in south London had only to stroll through the surrounding park to come across another such vision. A 'geological walk' revealed life-size sculptures of 'Extinct Animals' situated on islands surrounded by a lake (where they remain today), with an artificial cliff showing geological strata, and 'plantings' to evoke a primeval landscape (fig. 15). The sculptures by Benjamin Waterhouse Watkins (1807–94) were scaled up from small models whose making was supervised by the foremost palaeontologist of the day, Richard Owen (1804–92), soon to become Superintendent of the Natural History collections at the British Museum, and the driving force behind the creation of the Natural History Museum in South Kensington. The landscape created for the 'Extinct Animals' at Crystal Palace included living monkey puzzle trees (*Araucaria araucana*) and stone models of cycads (plants formed of a stout woody trunk and a crown of hard evergreen leaves).[17]

Cycads, found across tropical and sub-tropical parts of the world, until very recently were believed to be contemporary with the dinosaurs, as they were shown at the Crystal Palace. This was not the case; the extant species have evolved over a mere ten to twelve million years (as opposed to 230 million years), but their fascination for the Victorians was based on their status as 'living fossils'. James Yates (1789–1871), a Unitarian minister who in retirement devoted himself to scientific pursuits, kept the largest living collection of cycads in his palm house at Lauderdale House in Highgate, north London, as a complement to his geological study of the fossilized traces of Oolitic cycads found in Yorkshire. He donated his dried specimens of the foliage and fruits of the Cycadaceae to what was then the Botanical Department of the British Museum. *Araucaria araucana*, native to Chile and

16 'Ideal view of a marshy forest of the Coal Period': wood-engraving by Édouard Riou after Etienne Meunier in Louis Figuier, *The World before the Deluge*, London 1865, p. 139, pl. XI (British Library, London).

Argentina, belongs to another family of plants that was linked to a fossil predecessor from about 245 million years ago. It was introduced to Britain in 1795 by Archibald Menzies, a naval surgeon and plant collector who accompanied Captain George Vancouver on his circumnavigation of the globe in 1791–5. Menzies presented Sir Joseph Banks with seeds from which specimens were grown at Kew.

Victorians did not have to venture far afield to experience something of the eclecticism of Verne's subterranean scene. They encountered such luxuriance and sublime grandeur in the form of displays in the great glass houses that became a feature of private estates, botanic and winter gardens and international exhibitions. The first of these was Joseph Paxton's Great Conservatory at Chatsworth (1837), the seat of the Duke of Devonshire in Derbyshire. Decimus Burton's Palm House at Kew followed in 1848, and then the Temperate House, partially built by 1863 but not completed until 1898. In the United States the greatest example is the Garfield Park Conservatory in Chicago, built in 1906–7 to house whole landscapes. But the most famous of all these structures was Paxton's Crystal Palace, constructed in Hyde Park for the Great Exhibition of 1851, and moved to Sydenham in 1854. The *Illustrated Crystal Palace Gazette* claimed that, when mature, the plants brought to Sydenham from Florida, Java, India, Tahiti, South America and Australia would rival the Hanging Gardens of Babylon or the Garden of the Hesperides. Tiny oaks were even grown from acorns brought from Nineveh. The Nineveh Court, inspired by the Assyrian reliefs and sculptures recently acquired by the Louvre and the British Museum, was one of the major attractions until it was devastated by fire in 1866, along with many of the plants at the Crystal Palace.[18]

Alongside the exotic flora brought from abroad, and the glimpse they appeared to allow into an antediluvian age, was the fossil evidence of plant life that was emerging all the time from coalfields and quarries closer to home. This established the Carboniferous period (*c.* 360 million years ago) as the context for the emergence of the first trees. As another popular science writer, Louis Figuier (1819–94), wrote in *The World Before the Deluge* of 1865, 'from the study of fossils, science has not only reanimated the animals; it has reconstructed the theatre of their existence'.[19] He continued:

Sir Charles Lyell tells us that in Parkfield Colliery, South Staffordshire there was discovered in 1854, upon a surface of some hundreds of yards, a bed of coal which has furnished more than seventy-three trunks furnished with roots, some of them measuring more than eight feet in circumference; their

17 Diagram in the form of a tree, by Charles Darwin, in *On the Origin of Species by Means of Natural Selection*, London 1859, pp.160–61 (British Library, London).

Accompanied by eight pages of detailed explanation, this diagram was crucial to the successful communication of Darwin's evolutionary theory of how divergent species can trace their descent from a common ancestry.

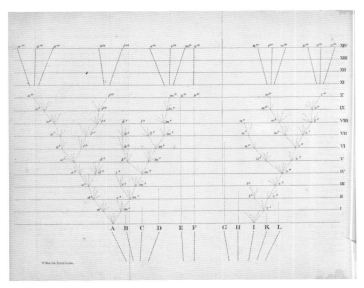

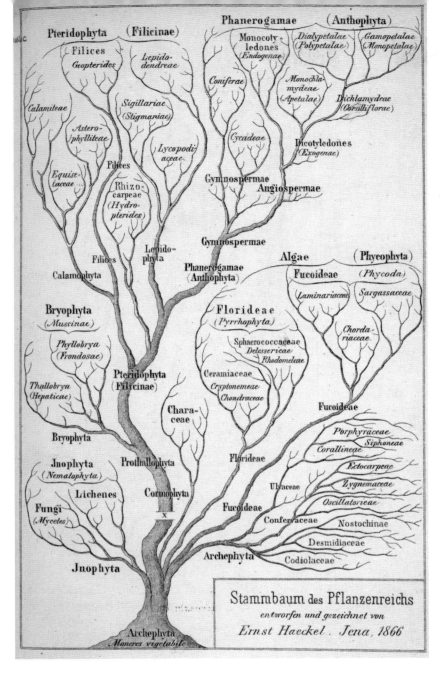

roots form part of a bed of coal more than eighty feet thick, resting on an argillaceous bed two inches thick, under which was a second forest superposed on a band of coal from two to five feet thick. Underneath was a thick forest, with great trunks of *Lepidodendrons*, of *Calamites* and other trees.[20] [see fig. 16].

Lepidodendron was a member of the lycophytes, an extinct family that produced a range of forest trees lasting into the Permian period 270 million years ago; the tallest could grow up to forty-five metres high. Outside the Natural History Museum in London are exhibited parts of the trunk of a fossilized tree around 330 million years old, unearthed in 1854 from Craigleath Quarry in Edinburgh. This is of the same vintage as the eleven tree stumps of Fossil Grove, discovered during the making of Glasgow's Victoria Park in 1887, one of the best surviving Carboniferous forest examples *in situ*.[21]

The tree that truly revolutionized the entire study of natural history was a conceptual one, first expressed in a rudimentary sketch of 1837, then in the form of an expanded diagram as the sole illustration to *On the Origin of Species by Means of Natural Selection* in 1859 (fig. 17) to express the diversification of species through natural selection from a common ancestry: 'The affinities of all beings of the same class have sometimes been represented by a great tree. I believe this simile largely speaks the truth'.[22] The motif became a commonplace of biological science, sometimes depicted more literally as an actual tree (fig. 18), but one that continues to change shape as befits its organic terms of reference.

27

CHAPTER TWO

MYTH
&
METAPHOR

MYTH & METAPHOR

THE concept of 'evolution' set out by Charles Darwin was soon applied to the mental and cultural development of mankind. Animism, the belief that spirits can reside in animals or features of the landscape, was interpreted as the first step towards the more sophisticated intellectual formulation of what might be termed 'religion', while folk and fairy tales were valued for providing insights into the 'primitive mind'.

The universal symbolism of trees was especially significant in the work of two writers, both of them Scottish. The first was Andrew Lang (1844–1912), whose many volumes of fairy tales, each denoted by a different colour, became a staple of children's literature in the twentieth century. The second was the anthropologist Sir James Frazer (1854–1941), whose most famous work, *The Golden Bough* (1890), was a wide-ranging exploration of comparative myth, religion and ritual. Frazer's title and frontispiece were taken from a painting by J.M.W. Turner (1834; Tate), inspired by Virgil's *Aeneid* (see p. 7). Taking as his starting point Virgil's account of the founding of Rome, Frazer's opening chapter, 'The King of the Wood', was the model for mankind's negotiation between the natural and supernatural worlds. *The Golden Bough*'s influence was far-reaching, and can be seen in C.G. Jung's theory of archetypes in human psychology; in the poetry and prose of W.B. Yeats and D.H. Lawrence; and in the work of Mircea Eliade, the Romanian philosopher and authority on comparative religion. It was a rich resource for the archaeologist Sir Arthur Evans, soon to unearth the Minoan palace at Knossos, in his study *The Mycenaean Tree and Pillar Cult and its Mediterranean Relations* (1901).

Frazer's evolutionary thesis and his erasure of differences in time, place and culture have long been called into question. What remains undeniable is that trees afford a ready vehicle for the articulation of ideas by analogy:

> Human beings have by no means exploited the forest only materially; they have also plundered its trees in order to forge their fundamental etymologies, symbols, analogies, structures of thought, emblems of identity, concepts of continuity, and notions of system. From the family tree to the tree of knowledge, from the tree of life to the tree of memory, forests have provided an indispensable resource of symbolization in the cultural evolution of mankind.[1]

To this list might be added trees of virtues and of vices, trees of folly, constitutional trees, liberty trees, trees of love, trees of peace, and many more besides. Several of these will be touched upon in the course of this book, but the most significant metaphor is the 'tree of life'. Although this term has a particular meaning in the Bible, it has been widely applied to any number of trees across many beliefs and cultures. It is sometimes used as a European construct applied to tree imagery in non-European cultures, at other times because the trees concerned are significant literally as the providers of the necessities of life, because they represent longevity or because they are part of a cosmology: 'The trees signify the universe in endless regeneration; but at the heart of the universe there is always a tree – the tree of eternal life or of knowledge.'[2]

Trees that are specially revered or regarded as sacred may be a particular species, for instance the date palm (*Phoenix dactylifera*) in ancient Mesopotamia and the types of fig tree important to different cultures and faiths: the sycomore fig (*Ficus sycomorus*) in ancient Egypt, the banyan (*Ficus benghalensis*) venerated by Hindus, and the peepal or bodhi (*Ficus religiosa*), Buddha's tree of enlightenment. Alternatively they can be generic, stylized motifs, such as the early depictions of sacred trees found on cylinder seals dating from *c.* 1700 BC, discovered in Syria.[3] The most striking examples of this kind of motif date from the reign of the Assyrian ruler Ashurnasirpal II (r. 883–859 BC), who built at Nimrud (modern Iraq) a palace containing 'halls of cedar, cypress, juniper, box-wood, meskannu-wood, terebinth and tamarisk'.[4] Magnificent gypsum reliefs from the throne room – brought to the British Museum in the mid-nineteenth century – show a 'sacred

19 Gypsum relief panel from the wall of the throne room in the North-west Palace of Ashurnasirpal II at Nimrud, 865–860 BC. 195 x 432.8 cm.

31

20 Shaman's drum made of reindeer skin stretched upon a wooden hoop, with designs painted on to the surface. Made by the Sámi people from arctic or sub-arctic Europe, 1500–1700. 39 x 33.5 cm.

Drums may have helped to induce the state of ecstasy necessary for the shaman to communicate with the spirit world. This drum was owned by Sir Hans Sloane, and formed part of the British Museum's founding collection.

21 Turquoise mosaic shield or disc, made with pine, resin adhesive and mosaic of turquoise and three types of shell, Mixtec, *c*. 1325–1521. Diam. 31.6 cm.

tree', thought to symbolize abundance and the fertility of the land. In the grandest of these (fig. 19), the king is depicted on either side of the tree, which is surmounted by a god rising from a winged sun-disc borrowed from Egyptian iconography. The two outer winged figures are protective deities performing a purification or fertilization rite, indicated by the cones and small buckets in their hands. In other panels the winged attendants have the heads of eagles, a classic Assyrian type of protective magical spirit.

The cosmic tree marking the *axis mundi* or centre of the world – uniting the sky with its branches, the earth with its trunk and the underworld with its roots – features in several belief systems from both the northern and southern hemispheres. It appears as Yggdrasil, the ash tree (*Fraxinus excelsior*), in the Norse sagas originally compiled in the thirteenth century (see p. 104). For the Sámi people of northern Scandinavia and north-western Russia the universe is comprised of three levels connected by the world-tree, which shamans ascend during their journeys of the soul (fig. 20). It was also a key motif for the Mexica (Aztec) people, who populated Central America prior to the Spanish conquest of 1519. A turquoise mosaic shield in the British Museum represents the principal divisions of the Mexica universe (fig. 21), showing a schematized tree whose trunk or 'world axis' emerges from the mouth of the earth goddess Tlatecuhtli. Its two main branches are split horizontally across the centre with flowers at the ends of the smaller ones. A serpent with a feathered tail coils upwards around the trunk, at the top of which is a reclining figure inside a teardrop-shaped cartouche; the serpent acts as an intermediary between the different layers of the cosmos, while the figure in the cartouche may refer to the belief, widespread in Mesoamerica, that a dynasty arises as if born from a tree.[5]

In China a most curious 'tree of life' is the subject of an episode in the Ming dynasty novel *Journey to the West* (Hsi Yu Ki), written by Wu Cheng'en in the 1590s. The narrative was based on the seventh-century pilgrimage made by the monk Xuanzang (Tang Tripitika Master) or to bring the sacred Buddhist texts from India to China. He and his companions, Su Wukong (Monkey), Zhu Bajie (Pig) and Sha Wujing, the river ogre (Friar Sand), arrive at:

. . . the Mountain of Infinite Longevity, and there was a Daoist temple on it called the Wuzhuang Temple. In this temple lived an immortal whose Daoist name was Zhen Yuan Zi. He was also known as the Conjoint Lord of the Age. The temple had a rare treasure, a miraculous tree that had been formed when primeval chaos was first being divided, before the separation of Heaven and Earth. In the four great continents of the world, only the Western Continent of Cattlegift's Wuzhuang Temple had this treasure that was known as 'Grass-returning Cinnabar' or 'manfruit' [ginseng, i.e. *Panax schinseng*]. It took three thousand years to blossom, three thousand years to form the fruit, and another three thousand years for the fruit to ripen, so that very nearly ten thousand years had to pass before the fruit could be eaten. Only thirty fruit were formed each ten thousand years, and they were shaped just like a newborn baby, complete with limbs and sense organs. Anyone whose destiny permitted him to smell one would live for three hundred and sixty years, and if you ate one you would live for forty-seven thousand years.[6]

As a mark of distinction Xuanzang is offered two of the manfruit, but he is horrified at the apparent invitation to cannibalism, failing to grasp that the 'babies' are the fruit of the sacred tree. His disruptive companion Monkey, incited by Pig, steals the remaining fruit, uproots the tree and generally wreaks havoc until compelled to seek

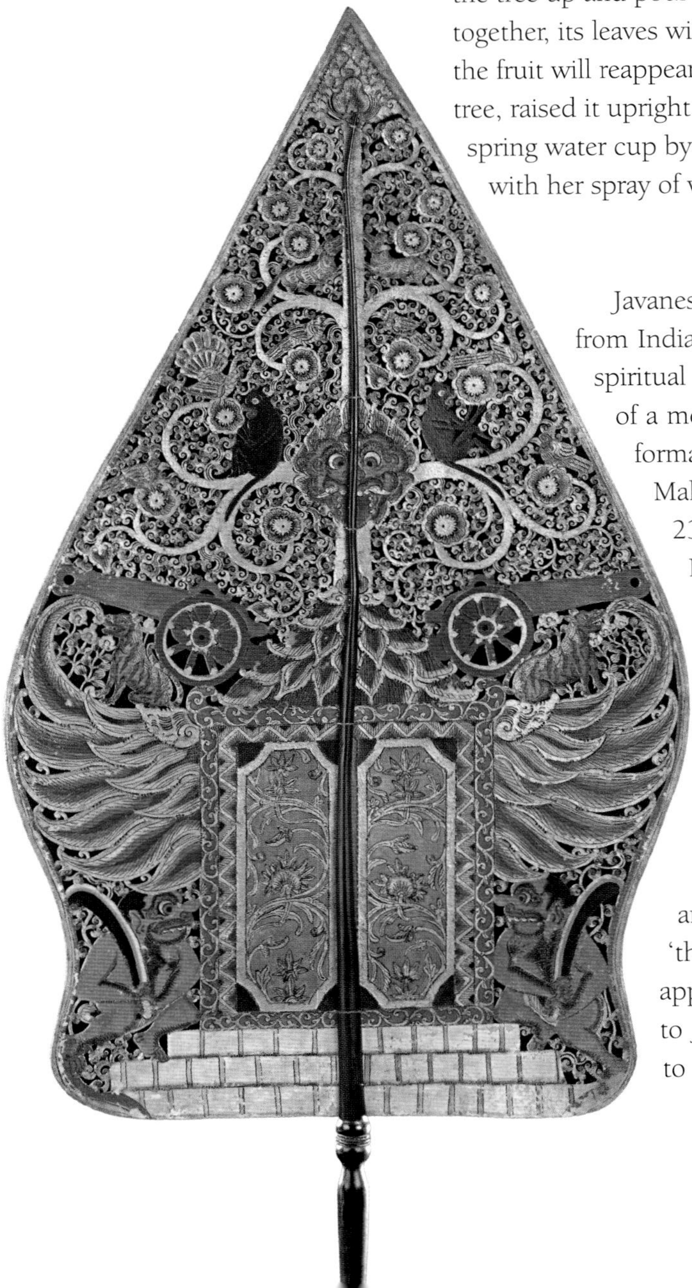

23 *Gunungan* or Cosmic Mountain: shadow puppet made of painted animal skin. Java, early 19th century. L. 99 cm.

redress. This is provided by Guanyin, the Bodhisattva associated with compassion, as shown in the seventeenth-century woodcut illustrated here (fig. 22):

> The Bodhisattva dipped her willow spray into the sweet dew in her vase, then used it to write a spell to revive the dead manfruit on the palm of Monkey's hand. She told him to place it on the roots of the tree until he saw water coming out. Monkey clenched his fist and tucked it under the roots; before long a spring of clear water began to form a pool. That water must not be sullied by vessels made of any of the Five Elements, so you will have to scoop it out with a jade ladle. If you prop the tree up and pour the water on it from the very top, its bark and trunk will knit together, its leaves will sprout again, the branches will be green once more, and the fruit will reappear. Monkey, Pig and Friar Sand put their shoulders under the tree, raised it upright, and banked it up with earth. Then they presented the sweet spring water cup by cup to the Bodhisattva, who sprinkled it lightly on the tree with her spray of willow and recited an incantation.[7]

Javanese (Indonesian) shadow puppet or *Wayang* theatre assimilated from India the cosmology of the tree that connects the physical and the spiritual worlds. *Gunungan*, a representation of the cosmos in the form of a mountain and a tree is always shown to open and close the performances, which draw largely from the two great Hindu epics, the Mahabharata and the Ramayana. The example shown here (fig. 23) was collected in the early nineteenth century by Sir Stamford Raffles, Lieutenant Governor of Java for the brief period of British rule from 1811 to 1816. In the trunk of the tree is a portal to the spirit world through which the puppet master (*dalang*), who acts as a kind of shaman or healer, can travel.

Across Anatolia and the Balkans the 'tree of life' was associated with longevity and rebirth; it was embroidered on clothing (fig. 24) and incorporated into wall- and floor-coverings including Islamic prayer rugs, which are intended to evoke Paradise. The fruit trees of the gardens of Paradise in the Qur'an are associated with heavenly bliss, but the most important tree is 'the Lote-tree of the farthest boundary' (*sidrat al-muntaha*), which appears in the Prophet Muhammad's night journey from Mecca to Jerusalem and then through heaven. On the spiritual journey to Allah no one may pass beyond this tree. Its botanical identity

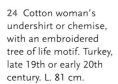

24 Cotton woman's undershirt or chemise, with an embroidered tree of life motif. Turkey, late 19th or early 20th century. L. 81 cm.

is a matter of debate; the Arabic name *sidr*, used in the Qur'an, is linked to *Ziziphus spina-christi* (Christ's Thorn jujube; see pp. 174–7), revered by Muslims and Christians in the Middle East.

THE TREE OF LIFE IN THE CHRISTIAN TRADITION

On the eve of the outbreak of the First World War, the psychiatrist Carl Jung experienced a series of recurring dreams. They were to signify a breakthrough in the development of his psychoanalytical theory of the concept of archetypes as images within the collective unconscious. The dreams were visions of apocalyptic destruction and desolation but with a redemptive ending:

> There stood a leaf-bearing tree, but without fruit (my tree of life, I thought),
> whose leaves had been transformed by the effect of the frost into sweet grapes full
> of healing juices. I plucked the grapes and gave them to a large, waiting crowd.[8]

25 ABOVE LEFT After J. Bakewell (fl. 1770s), *Hieroglyphicks of the Natural Man*, published by Bowles and Carver, London, 1790s. Hand-coloured engraving, 35.1 x 24.5 cm.

26 ABOVE RIGHT After J. Bakewell (fl. 1770s), *Hieroglyphicks of a Christian*, published by Bowles and Carver, London, 1790s. Hand-coloured engraving, 35 x 24.6 cm.

The Christian tradition that lies behind the metaphor of the 'tree of life', as dreamt by Jung, is rooted in the Old Testament – the fall from grace described in Genesis – and returns in the redemptive vision of the Revelation of St John the Divine at the end of the New Testament. The Garden of Eden, where it all began, was traditionally located in the land of Sumer, between the rivers Tigris and Euphrates, near modern Basra in Iraq ('Eden' is a Sumerian word meaning 'steppe'):

> And the Lord God planted a garden eastward in Eden . . . out of the ground made the Lord God to grow every tree that is pleasant to the sight, and good of food; the tree of life also in the midst of the garden, and the tree of the knowledge of good and evil . . . And the Lord God took the man, and put him into the garden of Eden to dress it and keep it. And the Lord God commanded the man, saying, Of every tree of the garden thou mayest freely eat: But of the tree of the knowledge of good and evil, thou shalt not eat of it: for in the day that thou eatest thereof thou shalt surely die.[9]

> And he shewed me a pure river of water of life, clear as crystal, proceeding out of the throne of God and of the Lamb. In the midst of the street of it, and on either side

of the river, was there the tree of life,
which bare twelve manner of fruits,
and yielded her fruit every month:
and the leaves of the tree were for the
healing of the nations.[10]

Religious and moral instruction was once
conveyed by emblematic or hieroglyphic
images, which depended on an understanding of visual analogies, although a
textual key was often provided as well. A
pair of single-sheet prints from the late
eighteenth century, *Hieroglyphicks of the
Natural Man* (fig. 25) and *Hieroglyphicks of a
Christian* (fig. 26), were meant to be 'read'
by the viewer in this way. The 'Natural Man'
is he who pursues material desires without
thought for salvation; his tree, rooted in
unbelief and watered by Satan and Death,
is therefore crooked and barren. It harbours
the serpent that tempted Eve, a reference to
the tree of the knowledge of good and evil
and the doctrine of original sin, as well as to

the fig tree that is fruitless because of the lack of repentance in the parable from the Gospel
of St Luke (13:6–9; see p. 99). The tree of the Christian, meanwhile, an allegory based on
the first of the Psalms, is truly the tree of life, rooted in Faith and Repentance with its verdant branches growing forth from the straight trunk of Hope and Love, while Satan is cast
out to the left. Another print from the same period called *The Tree of Life* (fig. 27) proved
to be one of the most popular of all such images, being continually adapted until well into
the nineteenth century. In the foreground the two prominent Methodist preachers, John
Wesley and George Whitefield, attempt to direct sinful revellers towards the narrow gate
to heaven and away from the gaping mouth of hell. The focal point of the composition is
the figure of the crucified Christ on the Tree of Life, set inside the redeemed Jerusalem, as
described in Revelation.

The image of Christ on the living tree goes back to medieval manuscript illumina-
tion of the thirteenth century[11] and the *Lignum Vitae*, a meditation by St Bonaventura of
c. 1260, which mentally maps the life of Christ upon the diagram of a tree: 'Picture in your
mind a tree whose roots are watered with an ever-flowing fountain that becomes a great
and living river with four channels to water the garden . . . From the trunk of this tree,
imagine that there are growing twelve branches that are adorned with leaves, flowers and

27 *The Tree of Life,*
published by Bowles
and Carver, London.
1790s. Hand-coloured
engraving, 35.3 x 24.9 cm.

28 William Blake (1757–1827), frontispiece (pl. 76) to the fourth and final part of *Jerusalem: The Emanation of the Giant Albion*. 1804–21. Relief etching, 22.2 x 16.1 cm.

fruit. Imagine that the leaves are a most effective medicine to prevent and cure every kind of sickness, because the word of the cross is the power of God for salvation to everyone who believes.'[12] The visionary poet and artist William Blake used the motif of the crucified Christ on the living tree for his frontispiece to the fourth and final part of *Jerusalem* (1804–20), the summation of his series of prophetic books which tells the story of the fall, captivity and ultimate redemption of mankind (fig. 28). This is done through the archetypal figure of Albion, who represents both mankind and Britain. As the narrative enters its concluding phase, Albion stands before the crucified Christ in an exultant attitude, signifying his final understanding of the meaning of Christ's sacrifice, which will allow him to enter the New Jerusalem.[13]

The tree of the knowledge of good and evil was co-opted for satire in a multitude of religious and secular contexts. James Gillray's print *The tree of Liberty,-with the Devil tempting John Bull* was directed against the siren call of Charles James Fox, Leader of the Whig Opposition in Parliament, to the British people to taste of the fruit of the tree of the knowledge of good and evil (shown as two separate trees) and follow the revolutionary example of the French (fig. 29).

29 James Gillray (1756–1815), *The tree of Liberty,-with the Devil tempting John Bull*. 1798. Hand-coloured etching, 37 x 26.8 cm.

Charles James Fox offers to John Bull the rotten apple of reform from the tree of the knowledge of evil, whose trunk of 'Opposition' is rooted in 'Envy, Ambition and Disappointment'. John Bull's preference is for the 'British' tree of the knowledge of good (in the background), whose trunk of 'Justice' supports branches of 'Laws' and 'Religion', bearing apples of 'Freedom, Happiness, Security' and 'Content'.

A MAPP SHEWING THE ORDER & CAUSES of Salvation & Damnation

By John Bunyan, Author of the Pilgrims Progress

Just as St Bonaventura structured his meditation upon a tree, so did others seeking to classify knowledge and direct the means of learning, whether for devotional or secular ends. The third-century Greek philosopher Porphyry presented the thought of Aristotle as a tree-like hierarchical scheme, engendering the diagrammatic 'Porphyrian trees' that were used for teaching logic until the nineteenth century. Joachim of Fiore (c. 1130/35–1201/2), the mystic theologian, biblical commentator and philosopher of history, visualized the culminating age of history as a series of flowering trees in his *Liber figurarum* (Book of Figures). Athanasius Kircher (1601/2–80), a German Jesuit priest fascinated by the 'oriental' languages and religions of the ancient world, designed a Kabbalistic tree in 1652 to illuminate the esoteric teaching of mystical Judaism,[14] while the Protestant Dissenter John Bunyan (1628–88) provided a diagrammatic *Map Shewing The Order & Causes of Salvation & Damnation* (fig. 30). Francis Bacon's metaphor of a tree of knowledge in *Of the Proficience of The Advancement of Learning, Divine and Human* (1605) was developed into a 'figurative system of human knowledge' by Diderot and d'Alembert, authors of the French *Encyclopédie* in 1751 (fig. 31), the defining work of the Enlightenment. The three main branches of the *Encyclopédie's* 'tree of knowledge' were Memory/History, Reason/Philosophy and Imagination/Poetry. Knowledge, including theology, was subject to human reason and not to divine revelation.

Charles Darwin's branching diagram in *On the Origin of Species by Means of Natural Selection* was an evolutionary tree with its origins in a further arboreal line of descent, the family tree, for Darwin saw the natural system as 'genealogical in its arrangement, like a pedigree'. The Western tradition for such pedigrees stems from the iconography of the Tree of Jesse, showing the ancestors of Christ: 'And there shall come forth a rod out of the stem of Jesse, and a Branch shall grow out of his roots.'[15] The genealogy itself is detailed at the beginning of the Gospel of St Matthew, the first book of the New Testament. It is represented here on an ivory panel from a casket probably made in Sri Lanka in the second half of the sixteenth century (fig. 32). Trading contact between

30 OPPOSITE *A Mapp Shewing The Order & Causes of Salvation & Damnation by John Bunyan*, engraved broadside printed by William Marshall. 1691. 42.5 x 32.4 cm.

31 RIGHT 'Figurative System of Human Knowledge', frontispiece from the first volume of *Encyclopédie*, 1751–65. (British Library, London).

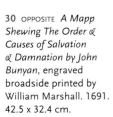

SYSTÈME FIGURÉ DES CONNAISSANCES HUMAINES.

41

32 TOP Ivory tree of Jesse. Possibly made in Sri Lanka, 16th century. 17.4 x 12 cm.

33 RIGHT Robert Peril (active first half of 16th century), The genealogical tree of the House of Hapsburg, twenty-two sheets joined together, beginning with King Pharamundo and ending with Emperor Charles V. Spanish edition 1540. Colour woodcut, L. (total) 734 cm; W. 47 cm.

Portugal and Sri Lanka from the early sixteenth century introduced Christian iconography even before some of the local rulers converted to the religion, such as the King of Kotte (modern Colombo) in 1557. Their adoption of Christianity created a demand for devotional objects for the new churches that were being built, as well as for export as luxury items to Europe. From the genealogy of Christ to that of the temporal rulers of the earth, the family tree became one of the most potent symbols of identity, status and legitimacy.

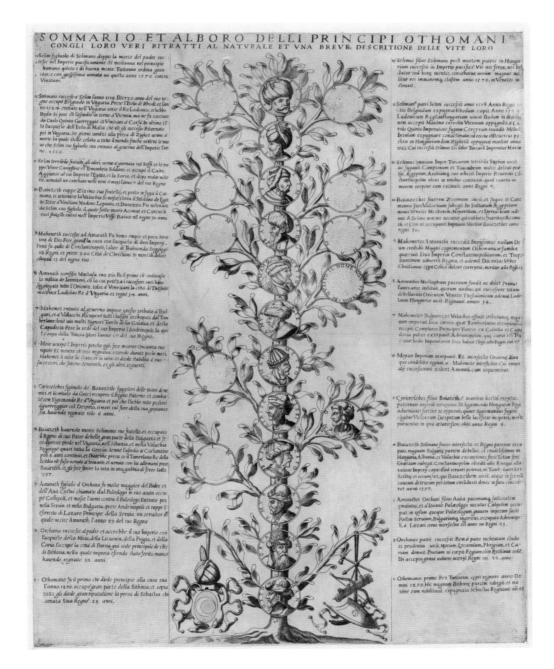

34 Genealogical tree of the Ottoman rulers from Othman I to Selim II. 1570. Engraving, 50.7 x 39.1 cm.

35 Agostino Carracci (1557–1602),
The Carracci family tree. After 1595.
Pen and brown ink, 28.9 x 20.3 cm.

The tree is shown outside the walls
of Bologna.

36 Ferdinand Olivier (1785–1841), dedication plate to seven places in Salzburg and Berchtesgaden. 1823. Lithograph, 28.2 x 35.5 cm.

The House of Hapsburg (fig. 33) and the Ottoman rulers in the sixteenth century (fig. 34) and then, at the turn of the sixteenth and seventeenth centuries, the Carracci family of artists from Bologna (fig. 35) are just a few examples. In the early nineteenth century the 'new-German religious-patriotic art', so-called by Goethe and his associate Heinrich Meyer, created its own pedigree in the form of an oak tree growing out of Dürer, who is represented on the trunk by an altarpiece adapted from his 1510 woodcut of the risen Christ from the *Large Passion* series (fig. 36). This family tree is more than just genealogical: it is also the Tree of Life, referring to the regeneration of German art.

THE TREE OF LIFE IN THE MODERN WORLD

There is no sign of the symbol losing its resonance in contemporary life. The film *The Tree of Life* (2011) written and directed by Terrence Malick, takes a live oak (*Quercus virginiana*) as its leitmotif within a drama of innocence, loss and possible redemption played out in Texas in the mid-twentieth century, intercut with scenes of the creation of the world. In London the British sculptor Rachel Whiteread, inspired by the Secession building in Vienna, has created a gilded 'tree of life' (2012) for the Whitechapel Art Gallery, to fill the upper façade of Harrison Townsend's art nouveau building of 1898–9.

Three objects from the British Museum's collection highlight the extent of the tree of life's global currency in the modern age. First, a printed cotton cloth, made to be worn as a woman's wrap (fig. 37), celebrates the Methodist Women's Fellowship of Ghana with the repeated motif of the Tree of Life and lines from the final verse of a favourite of the Methodist Hymn Book (no. 427), 'Through all the changing scenes of life' (Nahum Tate; 1652–1715). Next is a pottery candelabrum from Mexico (fig. 38), one of the many images produced annually for the Day of the Dead festival, celebrated on 1 November, All Souls' Day. Most remarkable of all, however, is *The Tree of Life*, made from decommissioned firearms by a group of artists working for the TAE collective (in English, Transforming Arms into Tools) in Maputo, Mozambique. Having purchased in 2002 another sculpture of this kind, *The Throne of Weapons*, the British Museum with Christian Aid commissioned *The Tree of Life* in 2004 (fig. 39). It was displayed in the Museum's Great Court as part of *Africa 05*, a year-long programme celebrating African culture, before moving into the

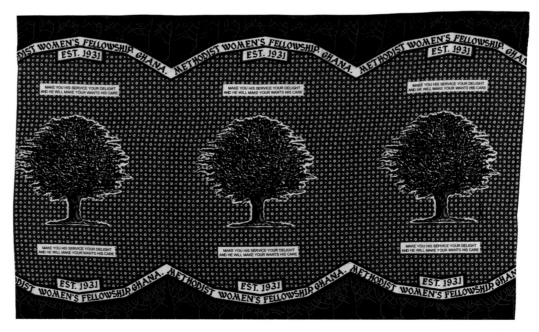

37 LEFT Cotton cloth for the Methodist Women's Fellowship Ghana, printed by Akosombo Textiles Ltd, Ghana, early 21st century. 170 x 110 cm.

38 OPPOSITE Tiburcio Soteno Fernández (b. 1952), pottery and wire tree of life candelabrum. Metepec, Mexico, 1980s. H. 102 cm.

Made for the Day of the Dead (Dia de los muertos) which falls on 1 November each year, the narrative takes place around a globe with an evolutionary path from ape to man and the stages of life from cradle to grave.

48

39 Kester (b. 1966), Fiel dos Santos (b. 1972), Adelino Maté (b. 1973) and Hilario Nhatugueja (b. 1964), *The Tree of Life*: metal sculpture. 2004. H. 300 cm.

As displayed in the Great Court of the British Museum in 2005.

Sainsbury African Galleries. The initial idea was to reference a specific tree of significance to Mozambique and other parts of Africa – the mango, baobab or cashew perhaps – but the final decision was to go for a symbolic one. TAE was founded in 1995 by Bishop Dinis Sengulane to encourage the voluntary surrender of weapons left over from the prolonged civil war that ended in 1992, in exchange for tools of production. Before the sculpture was shipped to London, it was set up in an open space in Maputo, known as Peace Park, and then in another part of Maputo, where political and religious leaders signed a commitment to peace beneath its branches on the National Day of Peace and Reconciliation.

ANOTHER PART OF THE WOOD

Ovid's *Metamorphoses*, completed at the beginning of the first century AD, inspired countless writers and artists to see the forest, its groves and particular trees as places of magic and transformation, notably Shakespeare and his 'Athenian wood' in *A Midsummer Night's Dream* (1595/6). The Roman poet's telling of the ancient Greek myth of Orpheus described how the sound of his music and poetry had the power to move nature, making the very trees draw near, among them oaks, poplars, limes, beeches, laurel, hazel, ash, firs, sycamore, maple, willow, box, tamarisk and myrtle. This created a paradigm for the artist who can conjure up the world in whatever form is desired, firing the imagination of the Austrian poet Rainer Maria Rilke (1875–1926). He composed his fifty-four sonnets to Orpheus in thirteen days in 1922, beginning with:

Tree arose from the earth. O pure ascendance –
Orpheus sings! O tall oak in the ear!
All was still. And then within that silence
He made the sign, the change, and touched the lyre.[16]

The Florentine Dante Alighieri (*c.* 1265–1321) inspired a literary and visual legacy to rival that of his Roman forebears, Virgil and Ovid. He made of the forest a metaphor for the human psyche, which he introduced at the beginning of the *Inferno*, the first part of his *Divine Comedy* (1308–21):

Midway along the journey of our life
I woke to find myself in a dark wood,
For I had wandered off from the straight path.[17]

By the end of *Purgatorio*, the second part of the *Divine Comedy*, the forest has shifted from an allegory for Christian guilt to become a terrestrial paradise. It is the setting for a vision of the triumph of the Christian Church and Dante's first sight of Beatrice, the real object

49

of his passion as well as the idealized figure of his imagination. The scene, replete with symbols from the Book of Revelation, including the Tree of Life, was brilliantly captured in one of the watercolours that William Blake made for *The Divine Comedy* (fig. 40). But neither this subject nor those described later in *Paradiso* have exercised the same hold as the scenes from hell, such as the wood of the suicides in the seventh circle:

> No green leaves, but rather black in colour,
> no smooth branches, but twisted and entangled,
> no fruit, but thorns of poison bloomed instead.[18]

Sin, in this case the mortal one of suicide, which was condemned by the Catholic Church as a rejection of the possibility of salvation, has corrupted nature itself. A 'genus' of malignant trees, poisoned or disfigured whether by human, divine or other supernatural intervention, can be traced back both directly and indirectly to Dante's metaphor, each successive image providing the opportunity for further grafting.

The Hanging, from Jacques Callot's series of prints *The Miseries and Misfortunes of War*, published in 1633, provided a compelling image of the tree as a locus of death, with its 'wretched fruit' suspended from the branches (fig. 41). The corpses are those of marauding soldiers hung in retribution for the devastation unleashed on Callot's native Lorraine during the Thirty Years War.[19] The motif appears on the reverse of a medal to mark the

40 William Blake (1757–1827), Beatrice on the Car, Mathilda and Dante (Purgatory, canto 29). 1824–7. Pen and watercolour over pencil, 36.7 x 52 cm.

41 Jacques Callot (1592–1635), *The Hanging*, plate 11 from *Miseries of War* (large format). 1633. Etching, 8.1 x 18.6 cm.

42 BELOW Erzsébet Esseö (1883–1954), cast bronze medal for the Hungarian Soviet Republic (reverse). 1919. Diam. 7 cm.

43 RIGHT Francisco Goya y Lucientes (1746–1828), *What a feat! With dead men!* plate 39 from *Disasters of War*. 1810–15, from the 1863 edition. Etching and drypoint, 15.5 x 20.5 cm.

abortive coup against the Hungarian Soviet Republic in June 1919 (fig. 42), and it may well have influenced the American sculptor David Smith for a detail in *Private Law and Order Leagues* (1939), one in his series of *Medals for Dishonour*.[20]

Callot's most important influence in this respect was on Goya, who echoed his title when choosing the final one for *Disasters of War*, the eighty-two etchings Goya worked on between 1808 and 1823 as a response to the events of the Napoleonic invasion of Spain and the Peninsular War from 1808 to 1814. *Disasters of War* was not published until 1863, long after his death, but the posthumous editions ensured its distribution. The plates have become an indelible iconography and indictment of man's inhumanity to man, none more so than that with the corpses and dismembered torso displayed upon the tree, with the ironic title *What a feat! With dead men!* (fig. 43).[21]

Dante's name was invoked constantly as the only adjective equal to conveying the visceral horror of the First World War battlefields of Belgium and France, where the 'wounded boughs' of the trees seemed 'as malignant limbs',[22] their mutilated remains standing sentinel for the amputated lives expended in the capture of often just a few yards of territory. The enormity of what was witnessed by war artists and writers on all sides, and the urgency of what they had to communicate, was expressed in works whose titles, *That cursed wood* (fig. 44) and *Void of war* (fig. 45), speak for themselves. Paul Nash, who created the latter image as a design for an exhibition poster, wrote to his wife of what he saw of the last phase of the Battle of Paschendaele in November 1917:

44 Christopher Wynne Nevinson (1889–1946), *That cursed wood*. 1918. Drypoint, 25 x 34.7 cm.

Nevinson served as a Red Cross ambulance driver before being invalided out in January 1916, then sent back to France in July 1917 as an official war artist. The title is a reference to a poem by Siegfried Sassoon, 'At Carnoy', dated 3 July 1916.

45 Paul Nash (1889–1946), *Void of war*. 1918. Lithograph, 37.1 x 44.4 cm.

I have just returned, last night, from a visit to Brigade Headquarters up the line, and I shall not forget it as long as I live. I have seen the most frightful nightmare of a country more conceived by Dante or Poe rather than by nature, unspeakable, utterly indescribable . . . the black dying trees ooze and sweat and the shells never cease . . . It is unspeakable, godless, hopeless. I am no longer an artist interested and curious, I am a messenger who will bring back word from the men who are fighting to those who want the war to go on for ever. Feeble, inarticulate, will be my message, but it will have a bitter truth, and may it burn their lousy souls.[23]

ART AND NATURE

In China the importance of landscape as a proper subject for artists had been assured since the Song dynasty (AD 960–1279), influenced by Daoism and the importance it attached to living in harmony with nature, as well as by Confucianism and Buddhism. A vocabulary of signs developed first in literature, then in the visual arts from the fourth century onwards. Trees were deployed within a framework of meaning that was not only accessible to an educated elite but also part of folk culture. Specific plants were associated with particular deities, Buddhist saints and Daoist Immortals; the four seasons and each month had its special flower, including flowering trees, as did all special occasions. An influential printed book of instruction for Chinese artists was the first part of the *Mustard Seed Garden Painting Manual*, published in 1679. Together with the remaining volumes, published in 1701, it was to be as important a source in Japan as it was in China (fig. 46).[24]

The status of landscape as a subject in its own right and the role that its composition could play in engendering the right effect, whether in terms of visual satisfaction or psychological projection, was keenly debated in Britain in the late eighteenth century. A change in attitude from the professional arbiters of artistic hierarchy was signalled in lectures given to the Royal Academy by the Swiss-born artist Henry Fuseli, when he invoked the authority of a pantheon of Old Masters – Titian, Salvator Rosa (fig. 47), the Poussins, Claude, Rubens and Rembrandt among them – to extol landscape that was not mere 'mapwork': 'Height, depth, solitude, strike, terrify, absorb, bewilder, in their scenery. We tread on classic or romantic ground, or wander through the characteristic groups of rich congenial objects.'[25] Trees offered great potential as 'characteristic groups of rich congenial objects'; their compositional value was immense, as demonstrated in the work of Rembrandt, whose etching *The three trees* of 1643 (fig. 48) was singled out for praise in this respect by J.M.W. Turner. The importance of understanding how to 'arrange' trees and how to make the most of their 'characters' – both individual and collective – was the focus of artistic instruction. There was a burgeoning literature directed at amateurs as well as those intent upon a professional career (fig. 49), for landscape drawing was seen as an appropriate arena for gentlemen and lady amateurs, by contrast with figure drawing, which was associated with formal academic training.

46 Wang Gai (1645–1707), after Shen Zhou (1427–1509), Allaying the summer heat under wutong trees (*Firmiana simplex* or Chinese parasol tree), from *The Mustard Seed Garden Painting Manual* (named after an estate in Nanjing). Woodblock print, 22.5 x 14 cm.

47 LEFT Joseph Goupy (1689–1769), after a lost painting by Salvator Rosa (1615–1673), *A rocky landscape with a blasted tree*. First half of the 18th century. Bodycolour, 18 x 22.3 cm.

48 BELOW Rembrandt Harmensz van Rijn (1606–69), *The three trees*. 1643. Etching with drypoint, 21.3 x 27.9 cm.

The canon of literature in English on this subject is framed by the work of William Gilpin (1724–1804), vicar of Boldre in the New Forest, and John Ruskin (1819–1900), both amateur artists. Gilpin's major work was *Three Essays: On Picturesque Beauty; on Picturesque Travel and on Sketching Landscape to which is added a Poem on Landscape Painting* in 1792, preceded by *Remarks on Forest Scenery and other Woodland Views illustrated by the Scenes of New-Forest in Hampshire* of 1791. The poem offers advice to the 'youthful artist':

> From mountains hie thee to the forest-scene
> Remark the form, the foliage of each tree
> And what its leading feature. View the oak
> Its massy limbs, its majesty of shade;
> The pendent birch; the beech of many a stem;
> The lighter ash, and all their changeful hues,
> In spring or autumn, russet, green or grey.[26]

The most significant exhortation is to assert the importance of being emotionally receptive to landscape before 'scientific employment' or 'the rules of art' intervene:

> We are most delighted, when some grand scene, tho perhaps of incorrect
> composition, rising before the eye, strike us beyond the power of thought . . .
> In this pause of intellect, this deliquium of the soul, an enthusiastic sensation

overspreads it, previous to any examination by the rules of art. The general idea of the scene makes an impression, before any appeal is made to the judgement. We rather *feel* than *survey* it.[27]

Gilpin's contemporary Uvedale Price (1747–1829) was a landowner whose *Essay on the Picturesque, As Compared with the Sublime and the Beautiful, and on the Use of Studying Pictures for the Purpose of Improving Real landscape* of 1794 was directed against the changes being wrought to many estates by the leading landscape designers of the age, Capability Brown and Humphrey Repton. He argued for a middle ground between nature and art, defining 'picturesqueness' as holding 'a station between beauty and sublimity',[28] but against a deadening uniformity and density of planting that gave rise to woods where no suicide would ever find room to hang himself, and 'clumps' of trees that 'placed like beacons on the summits of hills, alarm the picturesque traveller many miles off'.[29]

Work of a different emotional register was produced by the young Samuel Palmer (1805–81), who absorbed the literary influences of Virgil, the Bible and Bunyan and the artistic ones of William Blake and Old Master prints in the British Museum, including the work of Dürer and Lucas van Leyden, to which he was introduced by Blake's patron, the painter John Linnell. Palmer's sketchbook of 1824, acquired by the British Museum from a family descendant in 1964, is a unique record of this formative period of his life, when

50 Samuel Palmer (1805–81), study of trees, from a sketchbook. 1824. Brown ink, 18.9 cm.

The inscription, 'NB The chestnut ought to have/been in the middle', suggests the studies are based on direct observation.

art combined with direct observation of nature paved the way for his work in the 'valley of vision' in Shoreham in Kent from 1825 to 1835 (fig. 50).[30]

For Ruskin, the arch exponent of truth to nature, that truth had to be felt, not merely dissected; it was about 'the bond between the human mind and all visible things'.[31] As a young man he was taught by James Duffield Harding (fig. 51) whose *Lessons on Trees*, published in 1850, became a standard work. Though he praised Harding's dexterity and overall grasp of the 'energy of trees', Ruskin took him to task in *The Elements of Drawing* (1857) for insufficient appreciation of the individuality of each part of the foliage, which was every bit as important as the general impression. Ruskin's 'silvan' epiphany came when drawing an aspen tree (*Populus tremula*) in the forest of Fontainebleau in 1842, which revealed to him that the trees of the wood were more beautiful 'than Gothic tracery, more than Greek vase-imagery, more than the daintiest embroiderers of the East could embroider, or the artfullest painters of the west could limn'.[32] His artistic epiphany was his discovery of the work of J.M.W. Turner, for whom he wrote the first volume of *Modern Painters* (1843) as a polemic in his defence. For Ruskin, Turner's interpretation of landscape surpassed all others because of its 'incomprehensibility', its 'mystery, never to be fathomed or withdrawn'.[33]

Turner's late watercolour of Lake Nemi (*c.* 1840; fig. 52) is unfathomable in all the ways that Ruskin admired. Painted around the time when Ruskin first met Turner, it was

51 James Duffield Harding (1798–1865), A group of trees. *c.* 1850. Watercolour over graphite, 20.5 x 28.7 cm.

praised a few years later as the jewel in the crown of the notable collection belonging to Benjamin Windus at Tottenham in north-east London.[34] Lake Nemi, a volcanic crater known as 'the mirror of Diana', was a site of pilgrimage for every visitor to Rome since the seventeenth century, and the starting point for Frazer's *The Golden Bough*. Frazer substituted Lake Nemi and the sacred grove of Diana, goddess of hunting and the forests, for Lake Avernus near Naples, the legendary gateway to the underworld. Nemi and the ritual combat for the title of 'The King of the Wood' provided the beginning and the end of his study of 'theories of thought', 'a web . . . woven of three different threads – the black thread of magic, the red thread of religion and the white thread of science'.[35]

52 Joseph Mallord William Turner (1775–1851), *Lake Nemi.* c. 1840. Watercolour, 34.7 x 51.5 cm.

PART TWO

AN ARBORETUM

Baobab

Adansonia

THE BAOBAB is truly Africa's 'tree of life', on account of its phenomenal capacity to store water (one of its nicknames is 'bottle tree'), the fruit, seeds and leaves that are rich in nutrients such as calcium, iron, potassium and vitamin C, and the variety of uses to which its bark can be put when pounded, for example the making of rope, mats, baskets, paper, cloth and hats. Six of the eight species of baobab are indigenous to Madagascar, while a seventh – *Adansonia digitata* – also grows naturally on the mainland of the African continent, where it thrives in semi-arid regions. The eighth species, *Adansonia gregorii*, is indigenous to western Australia.

Adansonia digitata was the first species of baobab to be named by a European, the French naturalist Michel Adanson (1727–1806). He described it in his *Histoire Naturelle du Sénégal* in 1757, at which time the English common names for the tree were African Calabash tree or Ethiopian sour-gourd. It has become the emblem of Senegal, where tourists today can stay in hotels perched among the branches of baobab trees. *Adansonia digitata* grows in thirty other countries across the African continent, including South Africa, by the banks of Kipling's 'great grey-green, greasy Limpopo River'.[1] A specimen from the same region is often considered the largest example alive, with a circumference of nearly forty-seven metres. Such is the presence and power of the baobab that Thomas Pakenham, in his book *The Remarkable Baobab* (2004), mentions the 'funerals' sometimes granted to grand old trees or 'wooden elephants' as they are known.

100-franc banknote, issued by Banque de l'Afrique Occidentale, 1942. 7.9 x 13.8 cm.

The Bank of West Africa was founded in Dakar, Senegal, in 1901. Despite being a privately owned investment bank, it was authorized by the French Government to print currency.

BELOW
Decorated baobab nut from Kimberley, Australia, first half of the 20th century. L. 19.1 cm.

Seif Rashidi Kiwamba (b. 1977), *Urafiki wa mashaka*
(*Doubtful friendships* or *Friendship is gone*). 2002.
Enamel paint on wood, 100.3 x 96 cm.

Doubtful friendships is a product of the Tingatinga
Cooperative in Dar Es Salaam, Tanzania, a focus for the
popular art movement that had its roots in southern
Tanzania and the work of Edward Saidi Tingatinga
(1936–72), who painted on square wooden sheets in
enamel colours. Tingatinga subjects are often painted
many times in slightly different styles, always in pairs. The
companion piece to this work is *Friendship begins*, which
shows a 'wedding' between a tortoise and a zebra with
their animal guests in human clothing. In *Friendship is gone*
the same animals are eating each other, with the hollow
trunk of a giant baobab prominent in the background.
Intended to suggest the fickleness of human relationships,
these works have a particular significance in the light of
the ongoing tensions between Zanzibar and mainland
Tanzania, and between different groups of Maasai.

The baobab's singular features are the stuff
of legend and creation myths. The tree appears
to grow with its roots in the air, a characteristic
that prompted the missionary and explorer
David Livingstone (1813–73) to describe it
as 'that giant upturned carrot'. One African
explanation is that, when God made the world,
he gave each of the animals a tree. The hyena
was given the baobab but threw it away in disgust
so it landed upside down. Antoine de Saint-
Exupéry captured the tree's animated appearance
in his famous novella *The Little Prince* (1943), in
which the hero explains how he must constantly
strive to contain the baobabs on his tiny planet,
otherwise they will engulf and split it asunder.

The Australian name for the baobab is 'boab'; a song called *By the Boab Tree*
accompanies the closing credits of Baz Luhrmann's 2008 film *Australia*. The tree is thought
to have arrived on that continent as seeds which floated across the Indian Ocean from
Madagascar, and then to have spread inland from the coastal areas of western Australia.
Adansonia gregorii is only found in the Kimberley region of western Australia, though a few
specimens have crossed into the Northern Territory. The tree's seasonal changes enabled
aboriginal peoples to track the time of year, and accordingly it was known as the 'calendar
tree'. The fibres of the trunk were sucked to draw out moisture for drinking in times of
drought, and the nuts were used as a food source. With the growth of a tourist market, the
nuts have been turned into decorative items for sale, incised with naturalistic representations
of lizards, birds and other creatures, like the one illustrated here.

Birch

Betula

AROUND SIXTY SPECIES of *Betula* populate northern Europe, parts of North America and Asia, with a fossil history that dates back more than 65 million years. After the last major ice age across the North American and Eurasian continents, birch was an early colonizer in the advance of vegetation during the Mesolithic period (*c*. 10,000–*c*. 6000 BC), because of its ability to withstand extreme cold. The most important archaeological site of the Mesolithic period in Britain is at Star Carr in North Yorkshire, which was occupied from around 8770 to 8460 BC. Evidence has been found there recently for the oldest known dwelling in the United Kingdom, along with an 11,000-year-old birch tree trunk with its bark intact. Birch-bark rolls discovered during earlier excavations may have been used as net floats in fishing, in making containers, or as a source of resin. The bark is highly prized for its light weight and flexibility, while its resinous oil makes it almost imperishable.

A national birch collection for the United Kingdom has been established by the Royal Botanic Gardens Kew at Bethlehem Wood, Wakehurst Place, in Sussex, which aims to maintain a comprehensive representation of the different species from around the world. The species most commonly found in northern Europe are *Betula pendula* (silver birch) – once revered as a sacred tree with powers of renewal and purification – and *Betula pubescens* (downy or white birch). Bundles of birch rods from *Betula pubescens*, tied around an axe, formed the Roman symbol of authority known as the *fasces*, adopted by the American and French Republics in the late eighteenth century, and in 1919 as the emblem of Mussolini's National Fascist Party in Italy.

LEFT
Bronze figure of a lictor (magistrate's attendant) carrying laurel leaves in one hand and the *fasces* in the other. Roman, *c*. 20 BC– AD 20. H. 18.4 cm.

The *fasces* was the symbol of the power of the magistrates to impose either corporal punishment (with the rods) or capital punishment (with the axe).

ABOVE
Birch-bark rolls from Star Carr, Vale of Pickering, North Yorkshire, *c*. 8,500 years old. L. 6.2 cm.

Star Carr has been designated as a Scheduled Ancient Monument on account of its rarity and importance.

OPPOSITE
James Thomas Watts (1853–1930), *November evening in a Welsh wood*. *c*. 1904. Graphite and watercolour, 25.6 x 20.7 cm.

Born in Birmingham, Watts was deeply influenced by the writings of John Ruskin and the work of the Pre-Raphaelites.

LEFT
LEFT
Mide scroll, Grand Medicine Society, later coloured when in St Augustine's Missionary Museum, Canterbury. L. 35.1 cm.

One of a number of scrolls collected by Anglican missionaries before 1858 from 'Bad Boy', a Chippewa/Ojibwa from Minnesota. The Ojibwa were a woodland people of north-eastern America who migrated westwards to the Great Lakes region in the seventeenth century. These pictographic scrolls relate to the shamanistic beliefs of the *Midewiwin* or Grand Medicine Society, and the sacred stories of creation and migration, including many songs.

BELOW
Nest of thirty birch-bark baskets. 1725–40. H. 35 cm.

This rare nest of birch-bark baskets was made by the Cree people and probably acquired by Captain Christopher Middleton (d. 1770) in Hudson Bay, the centre of the fur trade in what is now northern Manitoba, Ontario and Quebec. Sir Hans Sloane, who bequeathed the nest to the British Museum as part of his collection, maintained a regular interest in the Subarctic and in the Hudson's Bay Company.

BELOW
Group of boxes and a miniature canoe, made by Odawa Native North American people from birch bark and porcupine quill. Before 1880. L. (canoe) 113 cm.

The development of the railroad system across North America brought tourism to places such as Niagara Falls and the Great Lakes and, with it, a market for Native American souvenirs. These items were among the Native American material brought back by Jesuit missionaries to Stonyhurst College in Lancashire, and later acquired by the British Museum in 2003.

66

Angelique Merasty (Cree, Saskatchewan, 1927–90/96), Cree 'bitten' design of leaves and birds. Birch bark, 20.5 x 16.5 cm.

Created by twice-folding a piece of thin birch bark and making symmetrical tooth marks.

67

Betula papyrifera is a species native to the northern United States and Canada. Two of its common names – paper birch and canoe birch – speak for themselves in terms of the practical uses to which the bark is put. In *Sylva* (see p. 19), John Evelyn mentioned a birch tree from Canada 'whose bark will serve to write on',[1] while Sir Hans Sloane had in his collection 'A Booke Made in Newfound Land of the Barke of Trees by Mr William Clerk Surgeon AD 1710' (now in the British Library). Evelyn also described how, 'In New-England our Northern Americans make canoos, boxes, buckets, kettles, dishes, which they sow, and joyn very curiously with thread made of cedar-roots, and divers other domestic utensils, as baskets, bags, with this tree, whereof they have a blacker kind'. In the epic poem *The Song of Hiawatha*, written in 1855 by Henry Wadsworth Longfellow, the hero calls upon the yellow birch, or *Betula alleghaniensis*, to surrender its bark for his canoe.

Birch-bark biting is an ancient skill among the Cree and Ojibwa, Algonquian-speaking peoples of the north-eastern woodlands in the Maritime provinces of Canada and northern New England, who also migrated westwards to the Great Lakes. The patterns and images created were used in story-telling and as stencils for quill- and beadwork.

68

In the poem *The Picture or the Lover's Resolution*, published in 1802, Coleridge wrote of the 'weeping birch (most beautiful / Of forest trees, the Lady of the Woods)', a characterization that is matched by the 'poetry' of Constable's drawing made nearly twenty years later. The same qualities inspired some of the finest writing of Robert Frost (1874–1963), the premier poet of the New England forest. *Birches* (1915) begins with the effects of an ice storm which has bent the trees so they appear 'Like girls on hands and knees that throw their hair / Before them over their heads to dry in the sun', moving on to a philosophical reflection on life and the yearning to begin anew as the 'swinger of birches':

So was I once myself a swinger of birches.
And so I dream of going back to be.
It's when I'm weary of considerations,
And life is too much like a pathless wood [. . .]
I'd like to get away from earth awhile
And then come back to it and begin over.[2]

69

Broussonetia papyrifera

BROUSSONETIA PAPYRIFERA played a major part in establishing the pre-eminence of east Asia in papermaking, which was already advanced in China by the second century AD, spreading to Korea and Japan over the next 2–4,000 years. The genus was named for the French naturalist Pierre Broussonet (1761–1807), while the species is closely related to other trees and shrubs commonly known as mulberry which belong to the genus of Morus (see p. 124), part of the family known as Moraceae.

The long-fibred inner bark of the paper mulberry tree produces a strong, pliable, soft paper that remains much in demand today. The German physician and naturalist Engelbert Kaempfer (1651–1716), who visited Japan in the employ of the Dutch East India Company in 1690–92, was the first European to describe the flora of that country. He wrote that, 'the Kozō or paper tree is a wild tree but because of its usefulness it is cultivated in the fields, where it spreads its branches with incredible speed and produces a lot of bark. With much pain and labour this is turned into paper, which, in turn, is made into match-cord, ropes, material, clothes and other things.'[1]

Broussonetia papyrifera facilitated the production of paper currency which was introduced in China in the seventh century AD. It was used by the Yuan dynasty (1261–1368) as the principal circulation, greatly impressing the Venetian traveller Marco Polo. Under the Ming dynasty (1368–1911), the paper appears to have been considered too fine for this purpose, with preference being given to the coarser variety made from the inner bark of *morus alba*, the white mulberry, which was otherwise cultivated for its leaves, the food source for silkworms.[2] The first detailed account of paper manufacture was included in *The Exploitation of the Works of Nature* (Tian Gong Kai Wu) written around 1637. *Hanji* is the name of the paper made from *Broussonetia papyrifera* in Korea which has been used since the

period of the Three Kingdoms (57 BC–AD 668) for all manner of ingeniously crafted items.

The tobacco pouch and fan shown here are but two examples of *hanji* applied to making domestic and immensely decorative objects. Tobacco was reputedly introduced by the Dutch in the early seventeenth century and pipe smoking soon became widespread, its prevalence commented upon by foreign visitors. The creative possibilities of *hanji* recently inspired a project in New York (June–July 2012), *Hanji Metamorphoses*, which brought together artists, fashion designers, architects and musicians.

In England by the middle of the eighteenth century, paper mulberry trees were being cultivated for their shade and decorative appearance from seeds sent from China.

LEFT
Tobacco pouch made of oiled paper mulberry bark. Korea, Chosŏn dynasty (1392–1897), before 1888.
This pouch and the fan pictured right were among the items donated to the British Museum by Thomas Watters (1840–1901), Acting British Consul General in Seoul around 1885.

71

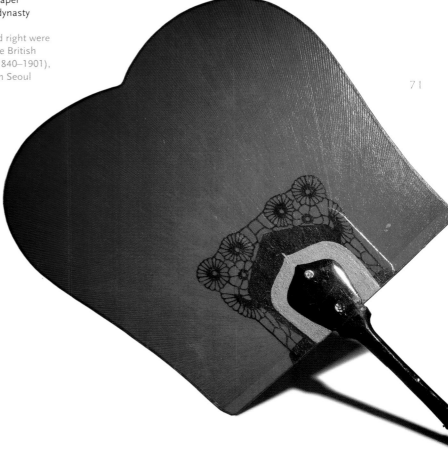

RIGHT
Fan made of paper mulberry bark, lacquer and bamboo. Korea, Chosŏn dynasty (1392–1897), before 1888. H. (with handle) 37.8 cm.

Fans were used in Korea by both men and women and often imitated the shape of natural forms such as the lotus.

OPPOSITE
Isoda Koryûsai (1735–*c.* 1790), *Paper mulberry tree and goat. c.* 1770–80. Colour woodblock print, 25 x 18.1 cm.

The paper mulberry tree (*kozō*) and long-haired goat (*muku-hitsuji*) appear on successive pages of a famous compendium of illustrations, *Ehon shaho-bukuro* (Treasure-bag of sketches) by Tachibana Morikuni (1679–1748), first published in Japan in 1720 and reprinted in 1770.

From the Eastern rim of the Pacific, the paper mulberry travelled to the islands of Polynesia and Melanesia, where it was used for making *tapa* or barkcloth (known in Hawai'i as *kapa*). Its importance for ceremonial purposes and as a commodity for exchange was immediately apparent to Europeans travelling to the Pacific in the eighteenth century. *A Catalogue of the different specimens of cloth collected in the three voyages of Captain Cook*, published in 1787, is proof of the interest that barkcloth aroused, as much for the different patterns created as for the material. Its production was – and still is – dominated by women, whose high status in Polynesia was reflected in the ritual significance of the barkcloth wrappings made for the bodies of living chiefs and for elaborately concealed images of gods.

The cloth is made from the inner bark of the paper mulberry tree, specially cultivated for this purpose since the nineteenth century. The bark is first softened by soaking it in water, and then pounded to make wide pieces that can be joined together with felt, bleached in the sun and decorated with vegetable dyes. *Tapa* became the main source of clothing on islands such as Fiji, Tonga and Tahiti, where it continues to be worn for ceremonial and festival occasions, as well as supplying a tourist market.

ABOVE
Katesa Schlosser (1920–2010), Portrait of Paresia holding on to the trunk of a paper mulberry tree. Savai'i, Western Samoa, 1978. Silver gelatin print, 30.4 x 20.3 cm.

OPPOSITE
Painted paper mulberry bark *tiputa* from Niue. Before 1866. 109 x 79 cm (without fringe).

Hiapo is the name used for barkcloth on the island of Niue in the southern Pacific, east of Tonga. The techniques of its manufacture and new kinds of garments, such as the Tahitian *tiputa* or poncho, were introduced in the 1840s by missionaries from Samoa who worked for the London Missionary Society. The decoration was entirely original to Niue. Most pieces date from the mid- to late nineteenth century and are now dispersed among collections all over the world, including four examples in the British Museum that came from the missionary Thomas Powell. He wrote an account of Niue in 1866 called *Savage Island* (the 'unofficial' name given by Captain Cook in 1774).

RIGHT
Photograph of Tongan adults working on *tapa* barkcloth. 1889–90. Glass negative, 12 x 16.4 cm.

Buxus

BOX GROWS in Europe, north-west Africa, Madagascar, Asia and the Americas, the most widespread of the European species being *Buxus sempervirens* (common boxwood). The largest native box woodland in Britain is at Box Hill in Surrey, at the summit of the North Downs, which has been renowned as a beauty spot at least since the seventeenth century. The slow growth of its wood leads to an exceptional density and hardness which renders it ideal for cabinet-making, scientific and musical instruments, small containers, chess pieces, general turnery, detailed carving, and as a matrix for printing. In Greek, *pyxos* means box, as in the shrub or tree, and *pyxis* a boxwood container, hence the term 'pyx', which is applied to the small vessels sometimes made of boxwood that were used to take the Holy Sacrament to the sick.

The special qualities of boxwood were exploited to the full in the making of this citole, a remarkable medieval musical instrument played like a guitar in so far as the strings were plucked with a plectrum. Some 250 years after its creation, the citole was altered to become a violin, an instrument lately introduced to the English court from Italy. The original parts are the back, sides and neck carved from a single piece of boxwood, the sides richly worked with forest scenes, including oak and hawthorn trees, and references to the labours of the months, such as the May rabbit hunt. When

BELOW
Citole, made of boxwood.
c. 1310–25. L. 61 cm.

OPPOSITE
Detail of the carvings on the side of the citole, showing a swineherd knocking down acorns to feed his pigs.

74

compared with manuscript illuminations, stone- and wood-carvings, the imagery has helped to date the work to the period 1310–25, when the citole is known to have been favoured at court during the reign of Edward II (1307–27). Its subsequent incarnation as a violin is associated with Robert Dudley, Earl of Leicester, and Elizabeth I, whose arms are engraved on the silver-gilt plate placed above the pegboard, along with the date 1578. This was the year of Dudley's secret marriage to Lettice Knollys; one theory is that the instrument was presented by him to appease the Queen, whose favourite he had been. The refashioning of the citole into a violin is likely to have been carried out by the Bassano family, notable instrument makers from Venice brought to London by Henry VIII, who was intent on bringing the musical standards of his court up to those of Italian and French counterparts.[1]

Along with ivory, boxwood was the preferred material for the microscopic carving that created sumptuous, miniaturized works of art for the private devotions of rich patrons in the late medieval and Renaissance period: rosary beads that contained whole narratives within them, and elaborate altars on a tiny scale, whose virtuosity was integral to their status as both religious and luxury articles.

The end grain of boxwood provided a perfect material for small-scale book illustration in the eighteenth and early nineteenth centuries. William Blake used this technique for the seventeen illustrations he made in 1821 for a school edition of *The Pastorals of Virgil*. In doing so he outraged the publisher, because the artist made his design appear as white against black, reversing the usual convention of black against a white background. The young Samuel Palmer (see p. 57) was captivated by the illustrations: 'They are visions of little dells, and nooks, and corners of paradise; models of the exquisitest pitch of intense poetry.'[2]

Miniature altar carved in boxwood with scenes from the Life and Passion of Christ. Flemish, 1511. H. 25.1 cm.

ABOVE

William Blake (1757–1827), woodblock engraved for printing an illustration to Ambrose Phillips's 'Thenot and Colinet. Imitation of Eclogue 1', in Robert Thornton's *The Pastorals of Virgil*. 1821. 34 x 73 cm.

LEFT

William Blake (1757–1827), Illustrations to Ambrose Phillips's 'Thenot and Colinet. Imitation of Eclogue 1', in Robert Thornton's *The Pastorals of Virgil*. 1821. Wood engraving, 15.7 x 8.5 cm.

A sheet of proofs printed on one page, before the woodblock was cut down into four separate blocks.

Cedrus

'TRUE' CEDARS belong to the Pinaceae family: Atlas (*Cedrus atlantica*), native to the Atlas mountains of Algeria and Morocco; Cyprus (*Cedrus brevifolia*); Deodar (*Cedrus deodara*), native to the western Himalayas; and Lebanon (*Cedrus libani*), native to Lebanon, Syria and Turkey. Some other trees commonly known as cedars belong to the family Cupressaceae (see p. 94), including the species of juniper native to the eastern United States, known as 'pencil cedar' because it was used as the casing for graphite.

Of the true cedars, *Cedrus libani* has enjoyed the greatest renown. In the epic of Gilgamesh (see p. 7), the hero makes the perilous journey to the cedar forest with his companion Enkidu. The forest is guarded by the ogre Humbaba, placed there at the behest of Enlil, the supreme deity in charge of the earth ('So to keep safe the cedars, Enlil made it his lot to terrify men'[1]):

> They stood there marvelling at the forest, gazing at the lofty cedars, . . . They saw the Mountain of Cedar, seat of gods and goddesses' throne. [On the] face of the mountain the cedar proffered its abundance, its shade was sweet and full of delight . . . He [Gilgamesh] slew the ogre, the cedar's guardian, . . . he went down to trample the forest. He discovered the secret abode of the gods, Gilgamesh felling the trees, Ekidu choosing the timber.[2]

Gilgamesh eventually attains wisdom, but before he does so his indiscriminate environmental abuse represents the start of a long history of the destruction of

Impression from a haematite cylinder seal showing Gilgamesh and Enkidu killing the kneeling giant Humbaba, guardian of the cedar forest. Found in southern Iraq, 1400–1300 BC. H. 3 cm.

BELOW
Segment of cedar wood, 900–700 BC. Excavated at Nimrud, cut and polished in the mid-19th century. L. 21 cm.

the great cedar forests of Mount Lebanon. The few remaining groves, 'The Cedars of God', were inscribed as a UNESCO World Heritage site in 1998. Cedar is documented as a vital article of trade from the third millennium BC among the kingdoms of western Asia, where it was listed in Mesopotamian royal inscriptions as an item of booty or tribute. The Egyptians were major consumers, as shown in the scene identified as 'cutting Lebanon trees for the Egyptians' on one of the reliefs from the palace of Sargon II at Khorsabad in northern Iraq (710 BC), now in the Louvre. With aromatic and preservative qualities, cedar resin was used for mummification and cedar wood for coffins, as well as in the preparation of medicines and for burning as incense.

The length of the timbers from cedar trees and the wood's resistance to termites made it a valuable building material for ships, palaces and temples, most famously King Solomon's Temple in Jerusalem (see the drawing by Giordano, overleaf). The depredations were such that the emperor Hadrian issued a decree in AD 123 for the protection of the cedars of Lebanon. In the seventeenth century John Evelyn invoked the history of the depletion of cedar to buttress his argument in favour of proper forest management:

> Josephus tells us, That the Cedar in Judea was first planted there by Solomon . . . But, as I am inform'd by a curious Traveller, there remaining now not above twenty four of those stately Trees in all those goodly Forests, where that mighty Prince set fourscore thousand Hewers at work for the Materials of only one Temple and a Palace, 'tis a pregnant Example what Time and Neglect will bring to ruine, if due and continual care be not taken to propagate Timber.[3]

Archaeological excavation of the citadels at Nineveh, Nimrud, Khorsabad and Balawat in the second half of the nineteenth century demonstrated the magnitude of the Assyrian monarchs' building ambitions, and the concomitant demand for cedar. This

Painted cedar wood coffin of Nekhtankh, from Deir el-Bahri (Thebes) in Middle Egypt. Middle Kingdom, 12th Dynasty (1985–1555 BC). L. 212 cm

The eyes are on a side that would have faced east so the dead person within the coffin could watch the sun rise.

was brought by Phoenicians from the eastern Mediterranean to provide beams for the rooms and armatures for doors and gates, of the kind described by Gilgamesh: 'I will make a door, six rods in height, two rods in breadth, one cubit in thickness, whose pole and pivots, top and bottom, will be all of a piece.'[4] An inscription found at Balawat describes how, in order to build a temple there to the god Mamu (the god of dreams), Ashurnasirpal II (884–859 BC) 'marched to Mount Lebanon (and) cut down beams of cedar, cypress (and) daprānu-juniper. I made fast the cedar beams over this temple (and) constructed cedar doors. I fastened (them) with bronze bands (and) hung (them) in its doorways'.[5] In 1878 Hormuzd Rassan excavated for the British Museum the Balawat Gates set up by Shalmaneser III (858–824 BC). The original bronze reliefs are displayed near a modern reconstruction of the monumental gates on which they would have been mounted.

At the end of William Shakespeare's play *Cymbeline*, when all is revealed, a soothsayer interprets the meaning of a mysterious tablet as a prophecy of good fortune:

> The lofty cedar, royal Cymbeline
> Personates thee: and thy lopp'd branches point
> Thy two sons forth; who, by Belarius stol'n,
> For many years thought dead, are now revived,
> To the majestic cedar join'd, whose issue
> Promises Britain peace and plenty.[6]

Shakespeare's knowledge of the tree would have been through biblical or classical sources, not actual acquaintance, as the cedar did not arrive in Britain until 1638. That year Edward Pococke, a scholar of Arabic at Oxford University, grew one from a seed brought back from Syria. By the late eighteenth century *Cedrus libani* was established as one of the most popular ornamental trees of the great parks, which were being planted with 'exotics' laid out by landscape designers such as Capability Brown. In 1683 four specimens were planted at the Chelsea Physic Garden (the Apothecaries' Garden, see p. 22),

Luca Giordano (1634–1705), Solomon receiving timber for the temple from the King of Tyre. *c.* 1695. Black chalk and grey-brown wash, 30 x 42.5 cm.

The Neapolitan artist made this drawing as a study for a series of paintings on the life of Solomon, commissioned for the Spanish royal palaces.

BELOW
William James Müller (1812–45), *The Apothecaries' Garden*. 1840. Watercolour, 30.9 x 49.4 cm.

Jacobus van Huysum (1687/9–1740), *Cedar*. Watercolour with bodycolour, 37.5 x 26.5 cm.

One of 141 drawings in an album of plants whose names were registered by the Society of Gardeners at monthly meetings from 1723. The members met in Newhall's Coffee House in Chelsea, near the Apothecaries' or Physic Garden, with the aim of compiling a complete catalogue of all foreign species growing in England.

of which two were felled in 1771, a third in the 1870s and the fourth in 1904; the latter two appear in William Müller's view of the garden in 1840. Under the direction of Philip Miller, chief gardener from 1722 to 1771, cones from the cedars of Lebanon produced seeds for the first time. This was sufficiently remarkable for Sir Hans Sloane to take a branch of nine cones to show the Fellows of the Royal Society in 1729. It must have been very similar to the cluster illustrated by Jacobus van Huysum for the Society of Gardeners, from an album that came to the British Museum as part of the Sloane Bequest in 1753.

Coconut

Cocos nucifera

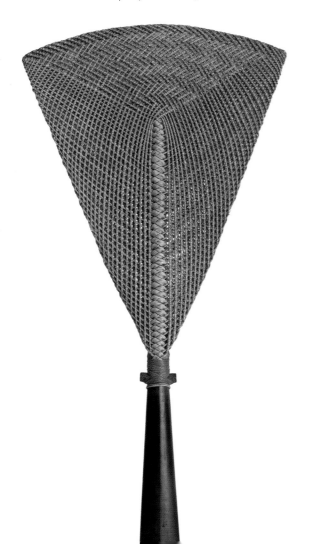

COCOS NUCIFERA, the only species of *Cocos*, belongs to the Arecaceae or palm family, one of the oldest and most diverse of all plant families. The multiplicity of its uses, embracing almost every part of the plant, has earned the coconut palm epithets such as 'the tree which provides all the necessities of life' in Sanskrit, 'the tree of a thousand uses' in Malay and the 'tree of life' in the Philippines.

The species is thought to have originated in the Indian Ocean. At the end of the thirteenth century Marco Polo was among the first Europeans to describe 'the Indian nut' (coconut), which he claimed to have seen in Sumatra, Nicobar, the Andamans, Madras and Malabar. The word 'cocos' did not appear in Europe until the beginning of the sixteenth century; it derived from *coco*, meaning 'grinning face' in Spanish and Portuguese, because of the three 'eyes' at the base of the coconut. Human agency, combined with the buoyancy of the coconut (which can withstand being carried by the tide for considerable distances to germinate elsewhere), has been responsible for the dispersal of the species throughout the tropics, to the Pacific, parts of the Americas, Madagascar and Africa. It reached West Africa via the Portuguese, once they had navigated a route to the Indies around the Cape of Good Hope at the end of the fifteenth century.

Brass plaque. Benin, Nigeria,
1500—1600. 50 x 37.5 cm.

This is one of the many
hundreds of plaques that
once adorned the walls of the
palace complex of the Oba,
the ruler of Benin.

Photograph of a coconut tree. Samoa, 1880. Albumen print, 10.3 x 6.2 cm.

BELOW
Kava drinking cup, made of coconut shell with an attached mouth wiper made of coconut fibre. Fiji, 19th century. Diam. 11.1 cm.

Kava (*Piper methysticum*) is ingested among the peoples of the Pacific for its sedative effect, either in ground form or as a drink. It has medicinal, religious, political, cultural and social purposes, and the objects associated with its preparation and consumption have a correspondingly important status.

European exploration of the Pacific in the eighteenth century provided evidence of the distribution and manifold uses of the coconut palm in this region. The Society Islands (named by Captain Cook), of which Tahiti (Otaheite) is the most important, appeared as an earthly paradise blessed with great natural beauty and an abundance of food, the coconut being prominent in both respects. It was a vital source of uncontaminated liquid for crews on the long sea voyages, as well as providing receptacles for other rations. The coconut shell used by Captain Bligh when he was set adrift following the mutiny on HMS *Bounty* in 1789 was acquired by the National Maritime Museum, London, in 2002. Two coconut plants are recorded as having been brought to Kew by William Bligh from Tahiti in 1793.

Further voyages in the nineteenth century documented the coconut's importance; for example, the *Narrative* of the 1857–9 expedition of the Austrian frigate SMS *Novara*, which circumnavigated the globe, reported that:

> At present [1857] the cocoa-palm is the sole plant which is cultivated by the natives of Kar-Nicobar [the most populous and northerly island in the archipelago of the Nicobar Islands]. It supplies them with all they require for food and lodging, for house-furniture, or for commerce with foreign peoples. The stem of this slender column . . . is yet stiff and strong enough to furnish cross-beams, laths, and masts for huts and boats. The fibres of the bark and of the nut-shells (known in commerce as Coir) supply cordage and line; the immense fan-shaped leaf . . . of the coronal serves as a covering for the roof, as also for plaited work and baskets. The juice of the nut . . . prevents the native from feeling even in the slightest degree the absence of available spring water, and is the sole beverage which invigorates and refreshes the wayfarer through these forest solitudes . . . The kernel of the ripe nut, thoroughly dried and pressed, gives forth a strong, clear, tasteless oil, which is used by the natives for anointing their skin and hair, and at the same time forms so important an article in European commerce, that above 5,000,000 ripe cocoa-nuts are annually exported through foreign mercantile houses in exchange for European fabrics.[1]

Artefacts from the Pacific caused a sensation when first displayed at the British Museum in the South Seas or Otaheiti Room, following the presentation by the Admiralty of the initial selection of items acquired on Cook's first two voyages in 1768–71 and 1772–5. The interest in Pacific cultures grew apace in the nineteenth and twentieth centuries through the activities of the many missionaries, colonial administrators and naval personnel to visit the region and, latterly, professional anthropologists. Fieldwork in the Pacific remains an important aspect of the British Museum's work, including the acquisition of contemporary material.

The dried flesh of the coconut from which oil can be extracted, known as copra, became particularly valuable in the mid-nineteenth century for the manufacture of soap, leaving a by-product for animal feed. Copra trading inspired Robert Louis Stevenson's novel *The Beach of Falesá* (1893), while the effects of coconut cultivation for this purpose formed part of his polemic *A Footnote to History: Eight years of Trouble in Samoa* (1892), written in response to the civil war across the Samoan islands, with Germany, Britain and the United States vying to fill the vacuum of power. Samoa's commercial economy was dominated by a German plantation company – 'a Gulliver among Lilliputs' as far as the islanders were concerned – where 'seven or eight hundred imported men and women toil . . . on contracts of three to five years, and at a hypothetic wage of a few dollars a month . . . You ride in a German plantation and see no bush, no soul stirring; only acres of empty sward, miles of cocoanut alley: a desert of food'.[2] The political outcome was not what Stevenson had recommended: the islands were partitioned between Germany and America in 1899, while Britain was compensated for relinquishing its claims with German concessions in Tonga, the Solomon Islands and West Africa.

The Philippines, Indonesia, India and Brazil are the biggest producers of copra today, but coconut is grown commercially in at least eighty countries, among them Papua New Guinea, the Solomon Islands and Vanuatu in the Pacific, Malaysia, the Maldives (where it is the national emblem), Mozambique, Tanzania and in West Africa.

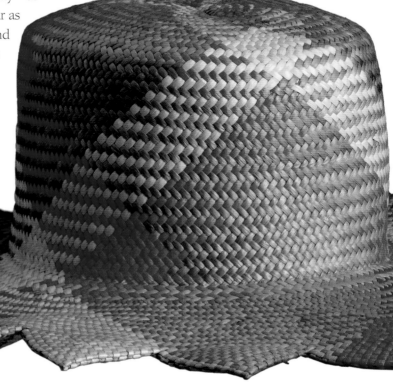

Crataegus

HAWTHORN belongs to a large genus of around a hundred species native to temperate regions of Europe, Asia and North America. It was widely used for hedges in medieval England, where the most famous thorn tree was the Glastonbury Thorn in Somerset. This is *Crataegus monogyna* 'Biflora', a variety of common hawthorn that flowers both in spring and in winter. The tree owes its special status to the legend of Joseph of Arimathea, who was venerated for retrieving the body of Christ from the Cross for burial. The legend emerged from medieval sources, but mention of the thorn tree does not appear until the early sixteenth century. According to an anonymous pamphlet of the late eighteenth century, which may have been known to William Blake:

> [Joseph] was appointed and ordained to go and preach the Gospel in England; and according as the mission commanded him, he took shipping at Joppa, and sailing with a great deal of difficulty, and meeting many dangerous storms, through the Mediterranean sea, he at length landed at Barrow-bay in Somersetshire, and then proceeding onwards of his journey eleven miles that day; came to Glastenbury in the same county; where, fixing his pilgrim's staff in the ground, it was no sooner set in the earth, but just like Aaron's rod (which blossomed flowers when there was a contest betwixt him and other learned Jews for the priesthood) it was presently turned into a blossoming thorn, which supernatural miracle made the numerous spectators, who came to see this wonder, be very attentive to hear his preaching the Gospel, which was concerning Christ crucified for the redemption of mankind.[1]

Mary Delany (1700–1788), *Crataegus oxyacantha* (now known as *Crataegus monogyna*), common hawthorn. 1776. Collage of coloured papers with bodycolour and watercolour on a black ink background, 24.1 x 19.4 cm.

The Glastonbury Thorn was cut down and burned as a relic of superstition by Cromwellian troops during the English Civil War, but was replaced by another, reputed to have been grafted from the original. A lively trade in cuttings for further propagation was reported in the early eighteenth century: 'There is a person about Glastonbury who has a nursery of them, who, Mr. Paschal tells us he is informed, sells them for a crown a peece, or as he can get.'[2]

After the Battle of Bosworth in 1485 Henry VII claimed the hawthorn tree as part of his insignia, because the crown of England worn by Richard III was supposedly taken and hidden in such a tree. But the hawthorn's most widespread association is with the festivals that announce the arrival of spring, especially the revels of May Day, which underwent many permutations, from the literary conventions of French medieval courtly romance to High Victorian reinvention of tradition. *The Court of Love*, an early sixteenth-century pastiche, once attributed to Chaucer, ends with the May Day service:

> Thus sang they all the service of the feast
> And that was done right early, to my doom;
> And forth went all the Court, both most and least,
> To fetch the flowers fresh, and branch and bloom;
> And namely hawthorn brought both page and groom,
> With freshe garlands party blue and white
> And then rejoiced in their great delight.[3]

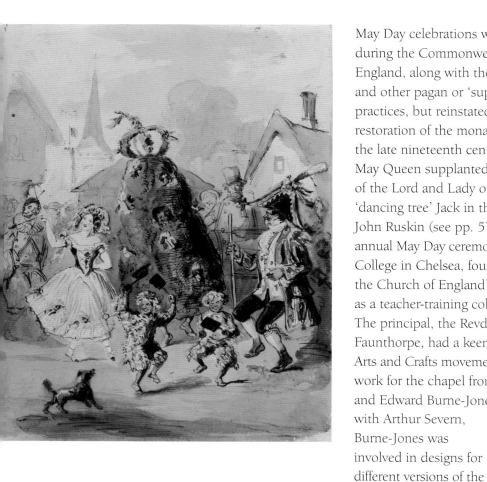

May Day celebrations were forbidden during the Commonwealth period in England, along with those for Christmas, and other pagan or 'superstitious' practices, but reinstated after the restoration of the monarchy in 1660. In the late nineteenth century the decorous May Queen supplanted the bawdy figures of the Lord and Lady of the May and the 'dancing tree' Jack in the Green. In 1881 John Ruskin (see pp. 57–8) inaugurated annual May Day ceremonies at Whitelands College in Chelsea, founded in 1841 by the Church of England's National Society as a teacher-training college for women. The principal, the Revd John Pincher Faunthorpe, had a keen interest in the Arts and Crafts movement, commissioning work for the chapel from William Morris and Edward Burne-Jones. Together with Arthur Severn, Burne-Jones was involved in designs for different versions of the 'Whitelands Cross', which Ruskin presented each year to the May Queen, elected by the students as 'the likeablest and the loveablest' of their number.

(see pp. 57–8)

May rituals across Europe were eagerly documented by folklorists and anthropologists such as Sir James Frazer (see p. 30) in the late nineteenth and early twentieth centuries. They were interpreted as evidence of residual belief in an animate nature, only in this case the spirits once thought to inhabit trees or other forms of vegetation had migrated into human beings. May Day's apotheosis came in 1890 when it was inaugurated as International Labour Day, on the back of a movement for an eight-hour working day, which began in the United States. It was first celebrated in Britain from 1891, Walter Crane's commemorative print bearing the exhortations, 'Wage workers of all countries unite! / The land for the people / Liberty Equality Fraternity'. Crane's love of the symbolism of nature prompted other work on the May Day theme, including *The First of May: A Fairy Masque*, written by his friend John Richard de Capel Wise (1831–90), with illustrations based on drawings Crane made during a visit to Sherwood Forest in Nottinghamshire. The book was published in 1881 with a dedication to Charles Darwin from the author and the artist.

(see p. 30)

LEFT
A Jack-in-the-Green procession, by an anonymous artist. *c.* 1840. Pen and brown ink and watercolour over graphite, 27.8 x 21.3 cm.

Jack in the Green dances along inside his framework of foliage, flanked by a king and a queen, with a jester in the background and two child chimney sweeps in front.

BELOW
Arthur Severn (1842–1931), *The Whitelands Cross*: gold cross in the form of flowering branches of hawthorn. *c.* 1887. H. 7.8 cm.

LEFT
Walter Crane (1845–1915), *May Day*, design for a greeting card. 1874. Watercolour and gold, 5.9 x 8.9 cm.

BELOW
Walter Crane (1845–1915), *The Triumph of Labour*. 1891. Woodcut, 34.2 x 81.3 cm.

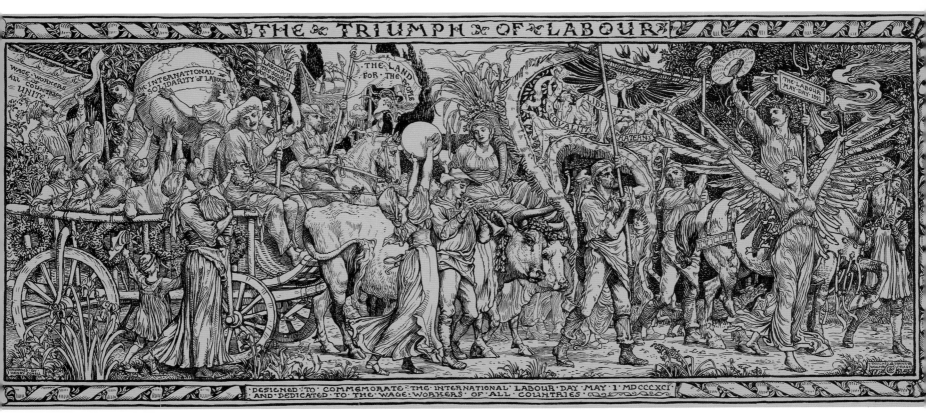

Cypress

Cupressus

'WITH the throng came the cypress, shaped like the cones that mark the turning point on the race-course: though now a tree, it was once a boy, dearly loved by the god who strings both lyre and bow.' Among the trees drawn by the music of Orpheus (see p. 49), Ovid names the cypress, formerly the boy Cyparissus, who unwittingly had killed a beloved companion, a stag sacred to the nymphs of Carthaea. In his grief Cyparissus begs the gods to be allowed to go on mourning for ever: 'Now, as his blood drained away, by reason of his endless weeping, his limbs began to change to a greenish hue, and the hair which lately curled over his snowy brow bristled and stiffened, pointing upwards in a graceful crest towards the starry sky. Sadly the god Apollo sighed: "I shall mourn for you", he said, "while you will mourn for others, and be the constant companion of those in distress."'[1]

Ovid's cypress tree was *Cupressus sempervirens* (everlasting cypress), commonly known as Italian cypress. It was not native to Italy but thought to have been introduced by the Etruscans from the Aegean and eastern Mediterranean, where it flourished in Cyprus, Crete, Greece, Turkey, Lebanon and Syria. Cypresses formed part of the sacred grove of Diana at Nemi, in the Alban hills outside Rome, and became a common signifier of the Italian landscape in artists' views (see p. 59). The tree's association with death has persisted from pagan antiquity until the present, when it continues to be in evidence in both Christian and Islamic graveyards.

Pliny gave a less than enthusiastic account of the tree: 'The cypress is an exotic, and has become one of the most difficult trees to rear, seeing that Cato has written about it at greater length, and more often than about all other trees, as stubborn to grow, of no use for fruit, with berries that cause a wry face, a bitter leaf, and a pungent smell: not even its shade agreeable and its timber scanty.'[2] He mentions other qualities that were the key to its widespread cultivation throughout the ancient world. Like cedar (see p. 78), its resistance to decay and aromatic oil made it important for all manner of building – some claimed it was the 'gopher wood' from which Noah made his ark – and for the burial of the dead. But it was the elegance of the flame-like trees and their decorative potential that made them the glory of gardens, from ancient Mesopotamia and Pliny's own villa

near Rome, to those of the Muslim rulers of Central and western Asia: Tamerlane's at Samarkand, which inspired Babur and his successors of the Mughal dynasty in northern India; the gardens of the Persian Safavids in Shiraz and Isfahan; and of the Ottomans on the slopes of the Bosphorus, after Mehmed II moved his capital to Constantinople/ Istanbul in 1457, and built the great palace of Topkapi Saray. The terraced gardens were laid out with cypress, planes, pine, willow and box; tile panels depicting cypresses from the early seventeenth century feature in the harem of the palace and in the Blue Mosque.

In Persian poetry the cypress was invoked as a simile of beauty in the opening lines to the Ruba'iyat of Omar Khayyam (1048–1131), and as an expression of love in the

Figure of a woman flanked by cypress trees, with flowers on the facing page, from *A briefe relation of the Turckes, their kings, Emperors, or Grandsigneurs, their conquests, religion, customes, habbits*, an album containing fifty-nine figures painted in watercolour with paper cut-outs of trees and flowers. 1618. 19.9 x 13 cm (each page).

The album bears the initials PM, quite possibly Peter Mundy (fl. 1600–1667), who left his native Cornwall in 1611 as a cabin boy on a merchant ship. In the course of his many travels he visited Constantinople, India, China and Japan.

LEFT
Prince in a garden, presented with a jungle fowl. *c.* 1590. Album leaf painted in bodycolour, 15.3 x 9.5 cm.

The subject is probably an episode in the life of the first Mughal emperor Babur (reigned 1526–30), whose memoirs were illustrated in 1589. The setting is a *chahar bagh* or paradise garden with four canals carrying water to a central pool, representing the four rivers of paradise in the Qur'an that were filled with milk, honey, wine and water.

OPPOSITE
Stone paste ceramic dish decorated with pheasants and a cypress tree. Made in Kirman (Iran), 1677/8. Diam. 40.5 cm.

Inspired by Chinese ceramics, which had long been imported into Persia, Kirman potters under the Safavid emperors (1501–1722) developed their own style for a domestic market.

poems of Shah Isma'il, founder of the Safavid dynasty, who wrote under the pen-name of Khatā'ī. For the song cycle *Cypress Trees*, composed in 1865 to woo his pupil, the actress Josefína Čermáková, Dvořák took the motif of the cypress from the love poetry of his Czech compatriot Gustav Pfleger-Moravský. The cypress as a symbol of freedom appealed to Henry Thoreau during his time alone in the woods at Walden Pond (see p. 18). In his reflections he quoted from the most famous work of medieval Persian literature, the book of wisdom known as *Gulistan* or *Flower Garden of Shaikh Sadi of Shiraz* (1259, translated into English by James Ross, 1823):

> The question is asked of a wise man as to why among all the celebrated trees God has created, only the cypress which bears no fruit is called 'azad' or free, to which the wise man replies: "Each has its appropriate produce, and appointed season, during the continuance of which it is fresh and blooming, and during their absence dry and withered; to neither of which states is the cypress exposed, being always flourishing; and of this nature are the azads, or religious independents. – Fix not thy heart on that which is transitory; for the Diljah, or Tigris, will continue to flow through Baghdad after the race of caliphs is extinct: if thy hand has plenty, be liberal as the date tree; but if it affords nothing to give away, be an azad, or free man, like the cypress."[3]

Cupressus sempervirens was introduced into England at the end of the fourteenth century, and by the middle of the seventeenth century was widely used for ornamental landscaping. The merchant and plant lover Peter Collinson (see p. 22) sent specimens in 1735 to his friend John Custis, the creator of a famous garden in Williamsburg, Virginia. Although this species is the most widely known, there are fifteen others within the genus that forms part of Cupressaceae, a conifer family which occurs all over the world. It includes junipers, swamp cypresses and the giant redwoods such as *Thuja plicata*, known as western red cedar, source of the wood used by Native Americans of the north-west coast for various kinds of carved poles, such as the two installed in the Great Court of the British Museum.

Jacques Le Moyne (1533–88), Cypress (*Cupressus sempervirens*) and Oak Eggar moth. *c.* 1585. Watercolour and bodycolour, 21.5 x 14.5 cm.

The artist Le Moyne accompanied an ill-fated French expedition to Florida in 1564 to record its findings. In 1581 he was granted letters of denization in England, where Sir Walter Raleigh and Sir Philip Sidney became his patrons. This watercolour comes from a group of fifty in the British Museum that were commissioned by Lady Mary Sidney, the mother of Sir Philip.

94

William Purser (1790–1852),
A Mohammedan funeral. 1820–30.
Watercolour, 16.7 x 24.7 cm.

Purser travelled extensively in Greece
and Turkey. Many of his views of
Constantinople/Istanbul were used
to illustrate travel books.

Eucalyptus

EUCALYPTUS has more species than any other tree apart from *Acacia*; all but fifteen of a total of around eight hundred are endemic to Australia. *Eucalyptus gummifera* or red bloodwood first struck Captain Cook and Joseph Banks in Botany Bay in 1770 because of the reddish gum that it yielded; seeds from this tree were among the few to survive the voyage on HMS *Endeavour*. The first actual specimen of a eucalypt, *Eucalyptus obliqua* (Australian/Tasmanian oak or Messmate stringybark), was sent from Australia to Europe in 1777, and seedlings were commercially available from a nursery in Kensington in London the following year.

European settlement of Australia from 1788 led to extensive clearance of eucalypt trees for agricultural land, but by the beginning of the twentieth century a growing awareness of their economic value led to better management and to reforestation. One of the great potentials of *Eucalyptus* arose from its medicinal properties, long known to indigenous peoples but developed for commercial exploitation in the mid-nineteenth century by Joseph Bosisto (1824–98), a pharmacist from Leeds who collaborated in Australia with the German botanist Ferdinand Müller (1825–96). In 1853 he succeeded in distilling eucalyptus oil from the Tasmanian blue gum (*Eucalyptus globulus*) and marketed it so successfully that one of the leading brands continues to bear his name today. The blue gum has become so widespread across Australia and the rest of the world that in some places it is regarded as an invasive species. By the end of the eighteenth century *Eucalyptus* seeds were being sent not only to Europe but also to India, then to South Africa, South America and the United States, especially California. The genus has become one of the most commonly planted forest trees, in demand for timber, pulpwood, high-grade charcoal for industrial use and – because of the trees' rapid growth – for land conservation.

In 1998 the Australian writer Murray Bail made *Eucalyptus* the subject of a novel of the same name. The main protagonist is a man who plants as many species as he can, from a desire to create order out of their 'chaotic diversity'. A tale of taxonomy, dissonance and re-enchantment unfolds, and the Linnaean names of different species of *Eucalyptus* punctuate the narrative, from *Eucalyptus obliqua* at the beginning to *Eucalyptus confluens* (Kimberley gum) at the end. The successful suitor for the hand of the man's daughter is not the one who passes the test of correctly identifying all the species growing on the property in New South Wales, but instead the man who – like the author – combines observation and exactitude with a gift for storytelling: 'So trees produced oxygen in the form of words.'

Conrad Martens (1801–78), 'Blue gum tree', from the set of twelve tinted lithographs *Sketches in the Environs of Sydney*. 1849. 22.8 x 17 cm.

Martens left England in 1833, joining HMS *Beagle* and Charles Darwin in South America for the voyage around the coast. He continued via Tahiti and New Zealand to Australia, where he spent the rest of his life, latterly taking the post of Assistant Librarian in the Australian Parliamentary Library.

LEFT
Eucalyptus globulus (Tasmanian blue gum) in the Australia Landscape at the British Museum, 2011.

Jimmy Moduk (b. 1942), *Yarrpany* (honey): painted coffin made from a eucalypt log. Ramingining, Northern Territory, 1980s. H. 152.3 cm.

Yarrpany-Dhuwa honey is one of four types produced by native Australian bees, as classified by the people of north-east Arnhem Land. Each type has its own creation story. The 1987–8 installation *200 Poles, The Aboriginal Memorial*, in the National Gallery of Australia, included these painted log 'coffins', made in Ramingining, to commemorate the loss of life sustained by indigenous peoples as a result of two hundred years of European settlement.

Fred Williams (1927–82), *Forest of gum trees*. 1965–6. Etching, 34.2 x 27.4 cm.

Fred Williams returned to Melbourne from London in 1958. His innovative treatment of the Australian landscape and short-hand notation for features such as the ubiquitous gum trees have become the lens through which many others now view that landscape.

For the indigenous peoples of Australia the eucalypts, in common with every other aspect of the landscape, have always 'produced oxygen in the form of words', and are symbols that constitute the Dreamtime myths and ways of being. Eucalypts provide food, medicine and shelter, as well as a habitat for the animals that contribute to their diet. They also hold cultural significance as the material for the didgeridoo, made from sections of wood that have been hollowed out by termites. The ritual purpose of eucalypts is strikingly evident in different mortuary practices. In some communities both living trees and trunks cut from the trees are carved to act as grave-markers. The people of Arnhem Land in the Northern Territory use hollowed-out logs as coffins, covered in the same totemic designs that are painted on the body of the deceased. Since the late twentieth century these coffins – like bark painting in general – have been produced for public display and sale, independently of their ritual function.

Ficus

The fig is a very secretive fruit.
As you see it standing growing, you feel at once it is symbolic:
And it seems male.
But when you come to know it better, you agree with the Romans, it is female.
　　　D.H. Lawrence, *Figs* (1923)[1]

FIG TREES rely on pollination by wasps, each of the nearly 850 species being dependent on its own particular wasp. John Evelyn, like Theophrastus and Pliny before him, described the phenomenon of 'caprification', whereby flower clusters from the hermaphrodite caprifigs, infertile specimens of the common edible fig (*Ficus caricus*), were hung from female trees to allow wasps to carry pollen from one to the other.[2]

Many species of fig flourish in the wild from Afghanistan to southern Europe, while the cultivation of *Ficus caricus* in particular has been documented for over four thousand years. Twenty-nine varieties of fig were mentioned in Pliny's *Natural History*: 'The figs that are highly approved are given the distinction of being dried and kept in boxes, the best and largest growing in the island of Iviza [Ibiza, one of the western Balearic isles known as 'the Isles of Figs'].'[3] The world's largest producers of the common edible fig today include Egypt, Turkey, Syria, Algeria, Morocco and the United States.

Pliny also wrote of the sacred tree in the Forum at Rome, where creatures struck by lightning were buried in homage to the fig tree under which Romulus and Remus, the founders of Rome, first sheltered on the Lupercal Hill. The fig is invoked along with the olive in one of the *suras* or divisions of the Qur'an. In the Bible it is the only tree to be named in the Garden of Eden, where the broad-fingered leaves of *Ficus caricus*

ABOVE
Charles Robert Leslie (1794–1859),
Ripe figs [*Ficus caricus*] in a bowl.
Mid-19th century. Watercolour,
10.8 x 15.3 cm.

C.R. Leslie was brought up in Philadelphia,
before establishing his career in London.
In 1843 he published the biography of his
friend John Constable.

LEFT
Oval basket of coiled palm fibre, containing
figs and dates. Egyptian, 18th Dynasty
(*c.* 1550–1292 BC). L. 20.2 cm.

provided the material for the 'aprons' sewn by Adam and Eve to cover their nakedness, once they had tasted the fruit of the tree of the knowledge of good and evil (see p. 36). This connection with original sin cast a blight over the tree's reputation in Christian texts. In the New Testament a barren fig tree serves both as a parable for lack of faith and as evidence of the power of faith, when Christ 'withers' a fig tree that he finds without sign of fruit. Most damning of all was its association with the suicide of Judas, following the betrayal of Christ. According to the Gospel of St Matthew, Judas hanged himself after returning the thirty pieces of silver to the temple. Hanging was regarded in the Roman world as being particularly shameful, and suicide of any kind was condemned as the work of the devil by the Christian Church at the Council of Arles in AD 425, because it was the rejection of God's mercy. The fig tree's unhappy association with Judas's suicide featured in an account from the end of the seventh century of a visit to the Holy Land by an Irish monk, who claimed to have seen the very fig tree itself.

The sycomore fig (*Ficus sycomorus*), principally found in tropical Africa, the Nile Valley and along the shores of the Red Sea to Israel, Jordan, Yemen and Oman, was one of the most useful and sacred trees of ancient Egypt. Valued for its shade, fruit and timber, and commonly mentioned in texts such as the Book of the Dead, it was used to make

ABOVE, LEFT
The Death of Judas and the Crucifixion: one of four panels from an ivory casket. Late Roman, *c*. AD 420–30. 7.5 x 9.8 cm.

Beneath Judas is the purse with the thirty pieces of silver given to him by the chief priests in exchange for leading them to Christ in the Garden of Gethsemane.

ABOVE, RIGHT
Urs Graf (1485–1527/8), 'The cursing of the fig tree', woodcut illustration to Matthias Ringmann, *Passio Domini Nostri Jesu Christi* (Strasbourg 1507). *c*. 1503. 24.4 x 16.5 cm.

One of twenty-five woodcuts illustrating Christ's Ministry and Passion, the subject was taken from the Gospels of Matthew and Mark. Christ pronounced that no fruit should grow on the fig tree, causing it to wither away, as proof of what the apostles could achieve if they remained steadfast in their faith.

furniture, represented on the walls and offering-tables of tombs of the 18th Dynasty (*c.* 1550–1292 BC) from Thebes, and found among food offerings for the dead, including those for Tutankhamun. The fruit of the sycomore fig is distinguished from that of the common fig by the incisions made to hasten ripening.

The Egyptian sky goddess Nut, associated with rebirth, is often depicted as the deity of the sycomore fig tree. She is portrayed in this way in one of the wall-paintings from the tomb of Nebamun, 'the Scribe and Grain-accountant in the Granary [of Amun]'. It depicts the 'garden of the west' in the afterlife, with a pool bordered by date palms (*Phoenix dactylifera*), heavily laden with fruit; dom-palms along the top (*Hyphaene thebaica*), which produce edible dom-nuts; sycomore figs, common figs and mandrake (*Mandragora*) bushes. Nut emerges from a sycomore fig at top right, offering her fruits to Nebamun (who is not visible in the fragment), to welcome him into the paradisaical garden.

Ficus caricus and *Ficus sycomorus* are among the species of fig trees that take root conventionally in the ground, but others – approximately half of the total number –

ABOVE
Mary Delany (1700–1788), *Ficus nitida*, 'shining fig-tree'. 1778. Collage of coloured papers with watercolour and bodycolour, 28.9 x 22.8 cm.

The species is now identified as *Ficus microcarpa var. nitida*, otherwise known as the Banyan fig, Taiwan ficus, Indian laurel fig, ginseng ficus or Chinese banyan. It was one of many exotic plants to which Mrs Delany had access on the estate of her great friend, the 2nd Duchess of Portland, at Bulstrode in Buckinghamshire, which was visited by Joseph Banks and Daniel Solander (see p. 10) in 1771. From 1776 George III and his queen regularly visited Mary Delany when she was at Bulstrode, observing the progress of her 'Hortus siccus' (see p. 10).

RIGHT
The pool in Nebamun's garden: tomb painting on plaster. Egyptian, 18th Dynasty, 1350 BC. 64 x 73 cm.

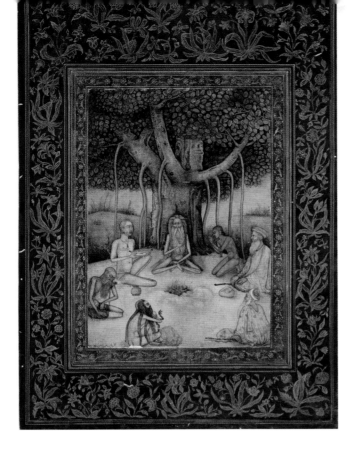

are epiphytic. This means they derive their moisture and nutrients from the atmosphere, sending down aerial roots to provide additional support for the canopy of branches above. In some of these trees, known as 'stranglers', the roots entwine the main trunk, but in others, such as *Ficus benghalensis*, the roots simply drop to the ground. The tenth-century Arab historian Mas'ūdī described the phenomenon as:

> . . . one of the marvels of nature and prodigies of the vegetable kingdom. It spreads over the ground with interlaced branches of the most beautiful appearance and richest foliage; it reaches up in the air to the height of the tallest palm trees, then its branches curve down in the opposite direction, forcing themselves into the earth . . . Then they reappear with new branches, which rise up like the first, descend and open a passage into the earth . . . If the Indians did not employ men to prune them, and for religious reasons having to do with the next life, look after these trees, they would cover the country, completely invading it.[4]

The name given by Europeans to this kind of fig tree, especially *Ficus benghalensis*, was banyan. This was taken from the Gujarati word 'banya', meaning merchant, because Hindu merchants would meet beneath the shade of these trees to conduct business. They were sacred places of meditation for Hindu ascetics or holy men (*Sadhus*), of whom Thomas Herbert wrote in 1634: 'Some of this Sect adore the Trees, and adorne them with Streamers of silke Ribands and the like.'

ABOVE, LEFT
Seven Hindu ascetics under a banyan tree (*Ficus benghalensis*), miniature painting in the Mughal style. 1630. 38 x 21.7 cm.

ABOVE, RIGHT
George Russell Dartnell (1799/1800–1878), 'Trunk of a banyan tree [*Ficus indica*] shattered by lightning – Coast of Malabar', from the album of drawings *Worthless Scraps from Many Lands*. 1828. Black ink, wash and white heightening, 18.2 x 24.1 cm.

A surgeon in the British army, Dartnell was posted to Sri Lanka, Burma and India from 1823 to 1832, recording the places he visited in this album of drawings. From 1835 he served in Canada, returning to Britain in 1843, where he became Deputy Inspector-General of Hospitals in 1854.

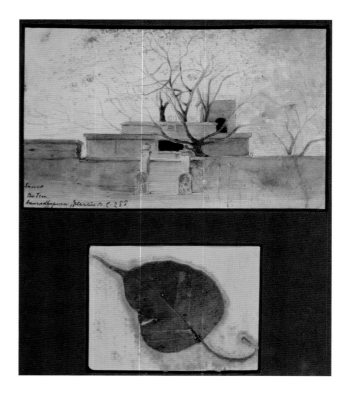

The most widely revered banyan of all is *Ficus religiosa*, the peepal tree or *ashvattha* in Sanskrit, and the Bodhi tree in Buddhism. The earliest depiction of a tree from India is of the peepal, shown on a seal from the Indus Valley civilization (3000–1700 BC). It is mentioned in the primary texts for Hindu philosophy and religion, the Vedas (*c.* 1500 BC, codified *c.* 600 BC) and Upanishads (fifth century BC); such was the peepal's status that to cut one down was considered a crime equivalent to killing a Brahmin or member of the priestly caste. For Buddhists the Bodhi tree is associated with the Buddha's meditation and supreme enlightenment (*bodhi*), which took place beneath the tree at the very end of the sixth century BC in north-eastern India at what became known as Bodh Gaya, 'the place of enlightenment'. The most important of the pilgrimage sites connected with the life of the Buddha, it contains the Mahobodhi Temple complex, reputedly founded by the Emperor Ashoka (reigned *c.* 269–232 BC), and the holy Bodhi tree. This was grown from a sapling from the Bodhi tree at Anuradhapura in Sri Lanka, said to have been propagated from the original Bodhi tree.

Another of the economic uses to which some species of fig tree lend themselves is the making of paper and bark cloth, an alternative to the paper mulberry (*Broussonetia papyrifera*) found in parts of Asia and Polynesia (see p. 70). One of these

(see p. 70)

ABOVE, LEFT
Painting on silk of the Buddha preaching in paradise beneath a jewelled Bodhi tree. China, Tang dynasty, AD 701–50. 139 x 102 cm.

This is one of the earliest and best preserved of the paintings found in 1907 in Cave 17 of 'the Caves of the Thousand Buddhas' on the Silk Road at Dunhuang in China.

ABOVE, RIGHT
Lt-Col Harry Hemersley St George (1845–97), The sacred bo tree at Anuradhapura (Sri Lanka), inscribed 'Leaves of the sacred bo-tree (Peepul of India) Anuradhapura – planted B.C. 288. Now 2177 years old picked 3.2.89 H.H. St. George.' 1889. Watercolour and bo tree leaf, 12.4 x 19.9 cm (mount).

Anuradhapura was the ancient capital of Sri Lanka where the Emperor Ashoka (reigned *c.* 269–232 BC) is credited with sending a branch from the Buddha's tree of enlightenment in order to spread Buddhism across the Indian sub-continent. The Bodhi tree at Anuradhapura is regarded as the oldest in the world.

poems of Shah Isma'il, founder of the Safavid dynasty, who wrote under the pen-name of Khata'i. For the song cycle *Cypress Trees*, composed in 1865 to woo his pupil, the actress Josefina Čermáková, Dvořák took the motif of the cypress from the love poetry of his Czech compatriot Gustav Pfleger-Moravský. The cypress as a symbol of freedom appealed to Henry Thoreau during his time alone in the woods at Walden Pond (see p. 18). In his reflections he quoted from the most famous work of medieval Persian literature, the book of wisdom known as *Gulistan or Flower Garden of Shaikh Sadi of Shiraz* (1259), translated into English by James Ross, 1823):

The question is asked of a wise man as to why among all the celebrated trees God has created, only the cypress which bears no fruit is called 'azad', or free, to which the wise man replies: "Each has its appropriate produce, and appointed season, during the continuance of which it is fresh and blooming, and during their absence dry and withered; to neither of which states is the cypress exposed, being always flourishing; and of this nature are the azads, or religious independents. – Fix not thy heart on that which is transitory; for the Dijlah, or Tigris, will continue to flow through Baghdad after the race of caliphs is extinct: if thy hand has plenty, be liberal as the date tree; but if it affords nothing to give away, be an azad, or free man, like the cypress."[3]

Cupressus sempervirens was introduced into England at the end of the fourteenth century, and by the middle of the seventeenth century was widely used for ornamental landscaping. The merchant and plant lover Peter Collinson (see p. 22) sent specimens in 1735 to his friend John Custis, the creator of a famous garden in Williamsburg, Virginia. Although this species is the most widely known, there are fifteen others within the genus that forms part of Cupressaceae, a conifer family which occurs all over the world. It includes swamp cypresses and the giant redwoods such as *Thuja plicata*, known as western red cedar, source of the wood used by Native Americans of the north-west coast for various kinds of carved poles, such as the two installed in the Great Court of the British Museum.

Jacques Le Moyne (1533–88), Cypress (*Cupressus sempervirens*) and Oak Eggar moth, *c.* 1585. Watercolour and bodycolour, 21.5 x 14.5 cm.

The artist Le Moyne accompanied an ill-fated French expedition to Florida in 1564 to record its findings. In 1581 he was granted letters of denization in England, where Sir Walter Raleigh and Sir Philip Sidney became his patrons. This watercolour comes from a group of fifty in the British Museum that were commissioned by Lady Mary Sidney, the mother of Sir Philip.

William Purser (1790–1852),
A Mohammedan funeral. 1820–30.
Watercolour, 16.7 x 24.7 cm.

Purser travelled extensively in Greece
and Turkey. Many of his views of
Constantinople/Istanbul were used
to illustrate travel books.

Eucalyptus

EUCALYPTUS has more species than any other tree apart from *Acacia*; all but fifteen of a total of around eight hundred are endemic to Australia. *Eucalyptus gummifera* or red bloodwood first struck Captain Cook and Joseph Banks in Botany Bay in 1770 because of the reddish gum that it yielded; seeds from this tree were among the few to survive the voyage on HMS *Endeavour*. The first actual specimen of a eucalypt, *Eucalyptus obliqua* (Australian/Tasmanian oak or Messmate stringybark), was sent from Australia to Europe in 1777, and seedlings were commercially available from a nursery in Kensington in London the following year.

European settlement of Australia from 1788 led to extensive clearance of eucalypt trees for agricultural land, but by the beginning of the twentieth century a growing awareness of their economic value led to better management and to reforestation. One of the great potentials of *Eucalyptus* arose from its medicinal properties, long known to indigenous peoples but developed for commercial exploitation in the mid-nineteenth century by Joseph Bosisto (1824–98), a pharmacist from Leeds who collaborated in Australia with the German botanist Ferdinand Müller (1825–96). In 1853 he succeeded in distilling eucalyptus oil from the Tasmanian blue gum (*Eucalyptus globulus*) and marketed it so successfully that one of the leading brands continues to bear his name today. The blue gum has become so widespread across Australia and the rest of the world that in some places it is regarded as an invasive species. By the end of the eighteenth century *Eucalyptus* seeds were being sent not only to Europe but also to India, then to South Africa, South America and the United States, especially California. The genus has become one of the most commonly planted forest trees, in demand for timber, pulpwood, high-grade charcoal for industrial use and – because of the trees' rapid growth – for land conservation.

In 1998 the Australian writer Murray Bail made *Eucalyptus* the subject of a novel of the same name. The main protagonist is a man who plants as many species as he can, from a desire to create order out of their 'chaotic diversity'. A tale of taxonomy, dissonance and re-enchantment unfolds, and the Linnaean names of different species of *Eucalyptus* punctuate the narrative, from *Eucalyptus obliqua* at the beginning to *Eucalyptus confluens* (Kimberley gum) at the end. The successful suitor for the hand of the man's daughter is not the one who passes the test of correctly identifying all the species growing on the property in New South Wales, but instead the man who – like the author – combines observation and exactitude with a gift for storytelling: 'So trees produced oxygen in the form of words.'

96

LEFT
Eucalyptus globulus (Tasmanian blue gum) in the Australia Landscape at the British Museum, 2011.

Conrad Martens (1801–78), 'Blue gum tree', from the set of twelve tinted lithographs *Sketches in the Environs of Sydney*, 1849. 22.8 x 17 cm.

Martens left England in 1833, joining HMS *Beagle* and Charles Darwin in South America for the voyage around the coast. He continued via Tahiti and New Zealand to Australia, where he spent the rest of his life, latterly taking the post of Assistant Librarian in the Australian Parliamentary Library.

For the indigenous peoples of Australia the eucalypts, in common with every other aspect of the landscape, have always 'produced oxygen in the form of words', and are symbols that constitute the Dreamtime myths and ways of being. Eucalypts provide food, medicine and shelter, as well as a habitat for the animals that contribute to their diet. They also hold cultural significance as the material for the didgeridoo, made from sections of wood that have been hollowed out by termites. The ritual purpose of eucalypts is strikingly evident in different mortuary practices. In some communities both living trees and trunks cut from the trees are carved to act as grave-markers. The people of Arnhem Land in the Northern Territory use hollowed-out logs as coffins, covered in the same totemic designs that are painted on the body of the deceased. Since the late twentieth century these coffins – like bark painting in general – have been produced for public display and sale, independently of their ritual function.

RIGHT
Fred Williams (1927–82), *Forest of gum trees*, 1965–6. Etching, 34.2 x 27.4 cm.

Fred Williams returned to Melbourne from London in 1958. His innovative treatment of the Australian landscape and short-hand notation for features such as the ubiquitous gum trees have become the lens through which many others now view that landscape.

LEFT
Jimmy Moduk (b. 1942), *Yarrpany* (honey): painted coffin made from a eucalypt log. Ramingining, Northern Territory, 1980s. H. 152.3 cm.

Yarrpany-Dhuwa honey is one of four types produced by native Australian bees, as classified by the people of north-east Arnhem Land. Each type has its own creation story. The 1987–8 installation 200 *Poles, The Aboriginal Memorial*, in the National Gallery of Australia, included these painted log 'coffins', made in Ramingining, to commemorate the loss of life sustained by indigenous peoples as a result of two hundred years of European settlement.

Ficus

Fig

The fig is a very secretive fruit.
As you see it standing growing, you feel at once it is
symbolic:
And it seems male.
But when you come to know it better, you agree with
the Romans, it is female.
D.H. Lawrence, *Figs* (1923)[1]

FIG TREES rely on pollination by wasps, each of the nearly
850 species being dependent on its own particular wasp. John
Evelyn, like Theophrastus and Pliny before him, described the
phenomenon of 'caprification', whereby flower clusters from
the hermaphrodite caprifigs, infertile specimens of the
common edible fig (*Ficus caricus*), were hung from female
trees to allow wasps to carry pollen from one to the other.[2]

Many species of fig flourish in the wild from Afghanistan
to southern Europe, while the cultivation of *Ficus caricus* in
particular has been documented for over four thousand years.
Twenty-nine varieties of fig were mentioned in Pliny's *Natural
History*.' The figs that are highly approved are given the distinction of being dried and
kept in boxes, the best and largest growing in the island of Iviza [Ibiza, one of the
western Balearic isles known as 'the Isles of Figs'].'[3] The world's largest producers of
the common edible fig today include Egypt, Turkey, Syria, Algeria, Morocco and the
United States.

Pliny also wrote of the sacred tree in the Forum at
Rome, where creatures struck by lightning were
buried in homage to the fig tree under which
Romulus and Remus, the founders of Rome, first
sheltered on the Lupercal Hill. The fig tree is
invoked along with the olive in one of
the *suras* or divisions of the Qur'an.
In the Bible it is the only tree to be
named in the Garden
of Eden, where the
broad-fingered leaves
of *Ficus caricus*

ABOVE
Charles Robert Leslie (1794–1859),
Ripe figs [*Ficus caricus*] in a bowl.
Mid-19th century, Watercolour.
10.8 × 15.3 cm.

C.R. Leslie was brought up in Philadelphia,
before establishing his career in London.
In 1843 he published the biography of his
friend John Constable.

LEFT
Oval basket of coiled palm fibre, containing
figs and dates. Egyptian, 18th Dynasty
(*c.* 1550–1292 BC). L. 20.2 cm.

provided the material for the 'aprons' sewn by Adam and Eve to cover their nakedness, once they had tasted the fruit of the tree of the knowledge of good and evil (see p. 36). This connection with original sin cast a blight over the tree's reputation in Christian texts.

In the New Testament a barren fig tree serves both as a parable for lack of faith and as evidence of the power of faith, when Christ 'withers' a fig tree that he finds without sign of fruit. Most damning of all was its association with the suicide of Judas, following the betrayal of Christ. According to the Gospel of St Matthew, Judas hanged himself after returning the thirty pieces of silver to the temple. Hanging was regarded in the Roman world as being particularly shameful, and suicide of any kind was condemned as the work of the devil by the Christian Church at the Council of Arles in AD 425, because it was the rejection of God's mercy. The fig tree's unhappy association with Judas's suicide featured in an account from the end of the seventh century of a visit to the Holy Land by an Irish monk, who claimed to have seen the very fig tree itself.

The sycamore fig (*Ficus sycomorus*), principally found in tropical Africa, the Nile Valley and along the shores of the Red Sea to Israel, Jordan, Yemen and Oman, was one of the most useful and sacred trees of ancient Egypt. Valued for its shade, fruit and timber, and commonly mentioned in texts such as the Book of the Dead, it was used to make

ABOVE, LEFT
The Death of Judas and the Crucifixion: one of four panels from an ivory casket. Late Roman, c. AD 420–30. 7.5 x 9.8 cm.

Beneath Judas is the purse with the thirty pieces of silver given to him by the chief priests in exchange for leading them to Christ in the Garden of Gethsemane.

ABOVE, RIGHT
Urs Graf (1485–1527/8), 'The cursing of the fig tree', woodcut illustration to Matthias Ringmann, *Passio Domini Nostri Jesu Christi* (Strasbourg 1507). c. 1503. 24.4 x 16.5 cm.

One of twenty-five woodcuts illustrating Christ's Ministry and Passion, the subject was taken from the Gospels of Matthew and Mark. Christ pronounced that no fruit should grow on the fig tree, causing it to wither away, as proof of what the apostles could achieve if they remained steadfast in their faith.

furniture, represented on the walls and offering-tables of tombs of the 18th Dynasty (c. 1550–1292 BC) from Thebes, and found among food offerings for the dead, including those for Tutankhamun. The fruit of the sycomore fig is distinguished from that of the common fig by the incisions made to hasten ripening.

The Egyptian sky goddess Nut, associated with rebirth, is often depicted as the deity of the sycomore fig tree. She is portrayed in this way in one of the wall-paintings from the tomb of Nebamun, 'the Scribe and Grain-accountant in the Granary [of Amun]'. It depicts the 'garden of the west' in the afterlife, with a pool bordered by date palms (*Phoenix dactylifera*), heavily laden with fruit: dom-palms along the top (*Hyphaene thebaica*) which produce edible dom-nuts; sycomore figs, common figs and mandrake (*Mandragora*) bushes. Nut emerges from a sycomore fig at top right, offering her fruits to Nebamun (who is not visible in the fragment), to welcome him into the paradisical garden. *Ficus carica* and *Ficus sycomorus* are among the species of fig trees that take root conventionally in the ground, but others – approximately half of the total number –

ABOVE
Mary Delany (1700–1788), *Ficus nitida*, 'shining fig-tree', 1778. Collage of coloured papers with watercolour and bodycolour, 28.9 x 22.8 cm.
The species is now identified as *Ficus microcarpa var.nitida*, otherwise known as the Banyan fig, Taiwan ficus, Indian laurel fig, ginseng ficus or Chinese banyan. It was one of many exotic plants to which Mrs Delany had access on the estate of her great friend, the 2nd Duchess of Portland, at Bustrode in Buckinghamshire, which was visited by Joseph Banks and Daniel Solander (see p. 10) in 1771. From 1776 George III and his queen regularly visited Mary Delany when she was at Bustrode, observing the progress of her 'Hortus siccus' (see p. 10).

RIGHT
The pool in Nebamun's garden: tomb painting on plaster. Egyptian, 1350 BC. 18th Dynasty, 64 x 73 cm.

them with Streamers of silke Ribands and the like.'

The name given by Europeans to this kind of fig tree, especially *Ficus benghalensis*, was banyan. This was taken from the Gujarati word 'banya', meaning merchant, because Hindu merchants would meet beneath the shade of these trees to conduct business. They were sacred places of meditation for Hindu ascetics or holy men (*Sadhus*), of whom Thomas Herbert wrote in 1634: 'Some of this Sect adore the Trees, and adorne them with Streamers of silke Ribands and the like.'

are epiphytic. This means they derive their moisture and nutrients from the atmosphere, sending down aerial roots to provide additional support for the canopy of branches above. In some of these trees, known as 'stranglers', the roots entwine the main trunk, but in others, such as *Ficus benghalensis*, the roots simply drop to the ground. The tenth-century Arab historian Mas'ūdī described the phenomenon as:

. . . one of the marvels of nature and prodigies of the vegetable kingdom. It spreads over the ground with interlaced branches of the most beautiful appearance and richest foliage; it reaches up in the air to the height of the tallest palm trees, then its branches curve down in the opposite direction, forcing themselves into the earth . . . Then they reappear with new branches, which rise up like the first . . . If the Indians did not employ men to prune them, and for religious reasons having to do with the next life, look after these trees, they would cover the country, completely invading it.[4]

The most widely revered banyan of all is *Ficus religiosa*, the peepal tree or *ashvattha* in Sanskrit, and the Bodhi tree in Buddhism. The earliest depiction of a tree from India is of the peepal, shown on a seal from the Indus Valley civilization (3000–1700 BC). It is mentioned in the primary texts for Hindu philosophy and religion, the Vedas (c. 1500 BC), codified c. 600 BC) and Upanishads (fifth century BC); such was the peepal's status that to cut one down was considered a crime equivalent to killing a Brahmin or member of the priestly caste. For Buddhists the Bodhi tree is associated with the Buddha's meditation and supreme enlightenment (*bodhi*), which took place beneath the tree at the very end of the sixth century BC in north-eastern India at what became known as Bodh Gaya, 'the place of enlightenment'. The most important of the pilgrimage sites connected with the life of the Buddha, it contains the Mahobodhi Temple complex, reputedly founded by the Emperor Ashoka (reigned c. 269–232 BC), and the holy Bodhi tree. This was grown from a sapling from the Bodhi tree at Anuradhapura in Sri Lanka, said to have been propagated from the original Bodhi tree.

Another of the economic uses to which some species of fig tree lend themselves is the making of paper and bark cloth, an alternative to the paper mulberry (*Broussonetia papyrifera*) found in parts of Asia and Polynesia (see p. 70). One of these

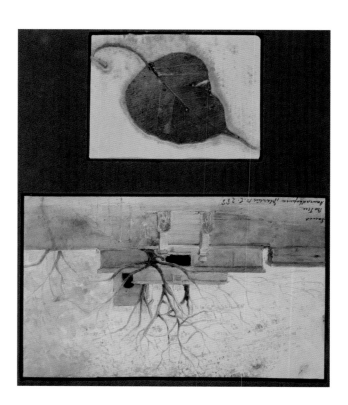

ABOVE, LEFT
Painting on silk of the Buddha preaching in paradise beneath a jewelled Bodhi tree. China, Tang dynasty, AD 701–50. 139 x 102 cm.

This is one of the earliest and best preserved of the paintings found in 1907 in Cave 17 of the 'Caves of the Thousand Buddhas' on the Silk Road at Dunhuang in China.

ABOVE, RIGHT
Lt-Col Harry Hemersley St George (1845–97), The sacred bo tree at Anuradhapura (Sri Lanka), inscribed 'Leaves of the sacred bo-tree (Peepul) of India) Anuradhapura – planted B.C. 288. Now 2177 years old picked 3.2.89 H.H. St. George'. 1889. Watercolour and bo tree leaf, 12.4 x 19.9 cm (mount).

Anuradhapura was the ancient capital of Sri Lanka where the Emperor Ashoka (reigned c. 269–232 BC) is credited with sending a branch from the Buddha's tree of enlightenment in order to spread Buddhism across the Indian sub-continent. The Bodhi tree at Anuradhapura is regarded as the oldest in the world.

species is *Ficus prolixa*, known as the Pacific banyan, while in Mexico a brownish paper is produced from the inner bark of *Ficus petiolaris*, an endemic species sometimes known as the lava fig. Its early use is seen in the painted codices of the sixteenth century, which provide a vital record of pre-Columbian history and belief at the time of the Hispanic Conquest. The Nahuatl word for this paper is *amatl*, which in turn has given its name to a contemporary art form, 'Amate art'. In Uganda the bark cloth is made from *Ficus natalensis* (natal or wild fig), a species of fig tree endemic in southern and eastern Africa. Bark cloth is historically associated with the Baganda people in central Uganda, and the skills were passed down from father to son, unlike the Polynesian tradition. Through recent community projects women have become involved in making and designing bark cloth to highlight contemporary issues.

LEFT
Sarah Kizza, 'United We Stand'
(translated from Swahili): bark
cloth hanging with raffia stitching,
pigment, cowrie shell and beads,
2008, 140 × 100 cm.

The bark cloth was made in
Kampala through the Design,
Health and Community Project,
supported by three university
partners in the UK, South Africa
and Uganda. It brings together
women from different craft groups
in Uganda to focus on the role of
design in health education – in this
case with reference to HIV/AIDS –
and economic advancement.

RIGHT
'Papers of Itzcuintepec': Mexican
codex, 16th century. Pigment on
fig-tree bark, 85 × 35 cm.

The codex is a cartographical and
historical record showing a mythical
place of settlement, early historical
dates and people migrating,
with about thirty-five locations
mentioned in the place signs.

Fraxinus

The use of Ash is (next to that of the Oak itself) one of the most universal:
It serves the Souldier . . . The Carpenter, Wheel-wright, Cart-wright, Cooper,
Turner and Thatcher . . . From the Pike, Spear and Bow . . . to the Plow; in
Peace and War it is a wood in highest request.

John Evelyn, *Sylva* (1664)[1]

THE ASH (*Fraxinus ornus*, sometimes known as the manna ash tree because of its sweet sap) was used to make spear shafts, the most celebrated being the spear of Achilles, with which he slew Hector and the Amazon queen Penthesilea in the battle for Troy: 'No other Achaean fighter could heft that shaft, only Achilles had the skill to wield it well: Pelian ash it was, a gift to his father Peleus presented by Chiron once, hewn on Pelion's crest to be the death of heroes.'[2]

In Scandinavia the ash acquired mythic status as Yggdrasil, the world tree in the poems and tales of Norse mythology known as the *Eddur*. There was intense literary and artistic interest in the medieval Norse sagas in the later part of the nineteenth century, championed in Britain by William Morris, who translated them from Icelandic.

Fraxinus excelsior (European or common ash) is the most widely found species of ash in many parts of Europe. An early and remarkably complete item made from this wood is a sword-sheath from the Iron Age fortifications at Stanwick St John in North Yorkshire, a stronghold of the Brigante tribe, whose territory extended over much of the north of England in the first century AD. Fragmentary evidence of the same wood has been found in connection with objects from many other archaeological sites in Britain, including the shield and buckets from the early seventh-century Anglo-Saxon ship burial at Sutton Hoo in Suffolk. But the Stanwick scabbard was exceptionally well preserved because it remained waterlogged in silt at the bottom of a defensive ditch, and was thereby deprived of the oxygen that causes decay.

Fraxinus americana (white ash or American ash), native across eastern North America, was first grown in Britain from seeds sent back in 1724 by Mark Catesby

Charles Ricketts (1866–1931), 'Yggdrasil', bookplate for Gleeson White. 1895. Woodcut, 17.5 x 15 cm.

Gleeson White was an art critic who in 1893 founded *The Studio*, an illustrated magazine which played an influential role in the Arts and Crafts movement.

Wooden sword-sheath, made from *Fraxinus excelsior*. Iron Age, AD 50–74, found at Stanwick, North Yorkshire. L. 73 cm.

The 1951–2 excavation at Stanwick in which the sword and scabbard were found was conducted by the eminent archaeologist Sir Mortimer Wheeler (1890–1976). The finds joined the 'Stanwick Hoard', discovered in 1843, a spectacular group of metal objects including a horse 'mask', that was already at the British Museum.

Black-figured pottery amphora (wine jar)
showing Achilles slaying Penthesilea, attributed
to Exekias (fl. 550–530 BC), c. 540–530 BC.
H. 41 cm.

Exekias was the most distinguished of all the
Athenian black-figure painters and potters, who
brought to the medium a strikingly original
interpretation of the Greek myths.

(1682–1749). Backed by Sir Hans Sloane and other
members of the Royal Society, Catesby completed
the first comprehensive survey of the flora
and fauna of the south-eastern area of North
America. In 1768 Philip Miller of Chelsea
Physic Garden wrote that, owing to demand,
Fraxinus americana trees were being grafted on
to common ash, because of their failure to
produce seeds in England. Together with
Fraxinus nigra (variously known as black ash,
brown ash, or hoop, swamp and basket ash),
from eastern Canada and the north-eastern
United States, including the Great Lakes
area, *Fraxinus americana* has been an
important source of materials and
medicines to Native Americans. It was used
for making smoking pipes, with stems
known as *calumets*, from the French
chalemel or *chalumeau*, meaning reed or
pipe. The smoking of tobacco and other
materials such as sweet grass and cedar bark
was a ritual part of ceremonies relating to
healing, prayers for rain, alliances and treaties
for trade, war and peace. A major collection of
Native American artefacts was amassed through
trade and exchange by Bryan Mullanphy, a late
eighteenth-century emigrant from Fermanagh in
northern Ireland, who made his fortune in America.
The collection accompanied his son to England in
1823, when the boy was sent to school at the Jesuit
college of Stonyhurst in Lancashire. It contained four
calumets, including a treaty pipe made of ash bearing the

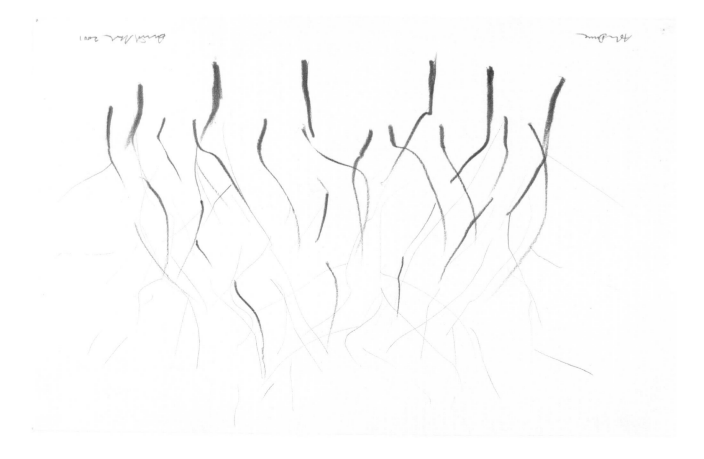

crest of the bald eagle, a sacred bird for many Native American peoples and a symbol of US Government since 1782.

The pliability and toughness of ash make it particularly well suited for timber frame structures, which are emulated in a 'living sculpture' by David Nash, an artist whose career has been dedicated to exploring the relationship between man and nature. His project *Ash Dome* began in February 1977, when he planted twenty-two saplings in Snowdonia, North Wales, with the intention of developing a domed space over thirty years. From 2001 to 2005 Nash produced a series of drawings that shows the trees growing into this shape. The environmentalist Roger Deakin (1943–2006) created his own ash bower in Suffolk in homage to David Nash's *Ash Dome*:

It consists of a double row of lively ash trees bent over in Gothic arches like a small church [one eighteenth-century theory was that Gothic architecture aspired to emulate the effect of an avenue of trees]. I planted it twenty years ago. . . . Years ago, once they had reached seven or eight feet, I bent the saplings together and grafted each one to its partner. They began to grow together, uniting into a single organism with two sets of roots but a single vascular system. . . . The result of all this wood-welding is a remarkably stable structure engineered in exactly the same way as a timber-framed house.[3]

ABOVE
David Nash (b. 1945),
Ash Dome, 2001. Graphite,
27.5 x 41.7 cm.

RIGHT
Pipe stem (*calumet*)
decorated with pictographs
including buffalo heads
and a bald eagle, made of
wood (ash), sinew, lead
and horsehair. Before 1825.
L. 114 cm.

John Constable
(1776–1837), Study of
an ash tree. 1823.
Graphite, 25.9 x 17 cm.

The drawing was made on
Hampstead Heath in north
London and is inscribed
by the artist, 'Hampstead
June 21. 1823. Longest day.
9 o'clock Evening. Ash',
showing his interest in
the different effects of the
seasons and the passage
of time.

Ginkgo biloba

THE GINKGO is a 'living fossil', and *biloba* (so-called for the bilobed shape of its leaves) is the only species to survive of the many that have been identified from the fossil record going back around 20 million years. Originating in China it has special associations with the Future Buddha, the Bodhisattva Maitreya, and with Confucius (551– 479 BC). These have led to the tree's cultivation in temples and shrines in China, Korea and Japan. The ginkgo was the most famous of the plants brought to the attention of Europeans by the German naturalist Engelbert Kaempfer (1651–1716; see p. 70), who first encountered the tree in Nagasaki in 1691: 'Another species of nut called *gin'nan* (ginkgo) has the shape of a large pistachio nut. It grows throughout the country on beautiful, incredibly large trees, with wide leaves shaped like those of the maidenhair fern, which is called *ich ō no ki*. The oil is used for many things.'[1] Kaempfer took ginkgo seeds back to Holland, where they were grown successfully at the Botanic Garden in Utrecht. More importantly, in 1712 he published a lavishly illustrated account of the plants he encountered on his travels from 1683 to 1693 through Russia, Iran, Arabia and Japan, which included the ginkgo and paper mulberry trees. *Amoenitates Exoticae* (*Exotic Pleasures*) attracted the attention of Sir Hans Sloane who, after Kaempfer's death in 1716, despatched George I's physician in Hanover to Kaempfer's hometown of Lemgo to purchase his manuscripts and collection of 'many natural and artificial curiosities'. These came with the rest of Sloane's collection to the British Museum in 1753, and are now divided between the Natural History Museum, the British Museum and the British Library. Furthermore, Sloane commissioned a translation of Kaempfer's unpublished manuscript *Today's Japan*, which appeared in 1727 as *The History of Japan*. Its reception was such that it had to be reprinted

Max Läuger (1864–1952), glazed earthenware tile with ginkgo leaf design. Designed *c.* 1900. 20.4 x 20.4 cm.

Läuger directed the art pottery division of the Kunsttöpferei Tonwerke Kandern (KTK) factory, near his hometown of Lörrach in south-western Germany, from 1895 to 1913. He produced highly original ceramics incorporating tree and plant motifs, often influenced by Iranian and east Asian decorative sources.

Gold-inlaid iron tsuba or metal disc in the shape of ginkgo leaves, for attaching as a handguard between a Japanese sword hilt and blade. 19th century. H. 7 cm.

LEFT
Ginkgo tree at the Royal Botanic Gardens, Kew, planted in 1762.

108

the following year, and was one of the books that Commodore Matthew Perry took with him in 1853 when he set out to open up Japan to the West.

Goethe was one of many writers and artists to be fascinated by the ginkgo. His poem *Gingo Biloba* was written for Marianne von Willemer, the object of his infatuation at the time. He sent his initial draft to her in September 1815, with two leaves attached from the ginkgo tree in the garden of the castle in Heidelberg, which they had visited together that month:

> The leaf of this Eastern tree
> Which has been entrusted to my garden,
> Offers a feast of secret significance,
> For the edification of the initiate.
> Is it one living thing
> That has become divided within itself?
> Are these two who have chosen each other,
> So that we know them as one?[2]

Japanese art and design had a huge influence in Europe in the second half of the nineteenth century. The ginkgo was one of the striking forms appropriated for the French decorative style of Art Nouveau and its German counterpart known as Jugendstil, lending itself to both naturalistic and geometric interpretation. The tree remains a powerful source of fascination, widely used in complementary medicine and an emblem of survival against all the odds because of its resistance to pollution. At Hiroshima four ginkgo trees at the epicentre of the atomic blast in 1945 are still growing today, while the earliest recorded example in Britain was planted at Kew in 1762 by the mother of George III. In 2005 the artists Gilbert and George (b. 1943 and 1942) produced twenty-five new works for the British Pavilion at the Venice Biennale, each incorporating images of the leaves of a ginkgo tree.

Kiyota Yûji (b. 1931), *Great Tree Ascending Like a Dragon*. 2000. Colour woodblock print, 103 x 72.5 cm.

This is one of several prints acquired from the same artist, three of which depict ginkgo trees at different Japanese shrines. 'At Furuno Shinmei Shrine, in the mountain village of Murômura, a giant, thousand-year-old ginkgo tree dominates the surrounding foliage and the impressions of visitors. Like the figure of a Guardian King, it defiantly twists and turns and spreads its branches, while reaching for the sky. Its vigorous strength recalls the torrent of vehement energy of a dragon ascending to heaven. Overflowing with life force, it transmits to the mountain village the will to thrive and prosper.' (Kiyota Yuji, *My Thoughts: To Commemorate Acquisitions by the British Museum*, 2004).

Guaiacum

LIGNUM VITAE is a tropical hardwood, the heartwood of the two species *Guaiacum sanctum* and *Guaiacum officinale*, which grow in the Caribbean, Florida, the Bahamas and parts of Central and South America. *Guaiacum sanctum* is the national tree of the Bahamas, and *Guaiacum officinale* the national flower of Jamaica. First introduced to Europe by Spanish explorers in the early sixteenth century, the wood was soon in demand for its strength, its oily, self-lubricating properties and its medicinal potential: the resin was variously used to treat respiratory problems, skin disorders, gout and syphilis, hence *Lignum vitae*, meaning 'wood of life'. For sailors and marine craftsmen, it provided excellent material for all manner of nautical instruments, moving parts such as gears and bearings, and ship-frame construction from the age of sail to that of steam and the submarine.

The Linnaean name for *Guaiacum officinale* was based on a drawing of one of the specimens collected by Hans Sloane when he was in Jamaica in 1687–9 as the personal physician of the Governor, the 2nd Duke of Albemarle. The visit lasted only sixteen months, but it had a transformative effect on Sloane's botanical knowledge and interests. In the second volume of his *Natural History of Jamaica* (1725), Sloane wrote of ironwood (another of the common names for *Guaiacum officinale*): 'This tree has a very hard Wood, of a pale yellow Colour, close like Box, cover'd with a grey Bark, rising to twenty Foot high, having numerous Branches spread on every Hand . . . *James Reid* brought a Tree over from *barbadoes* . . . he tells us, that 'tis proper to make Cogs, that neither Sun nor Wind hurts it, and that it is so hard as to break their Tools.' Sloane went on to provide the first full description of the medicinal properties of the species.

The most remarkable use of *Lignum vitae* was made by the Taino, the indigenous people whose territories stretched across the Bahamas and Greater Antilles (Cuba, Haiti, the Dominican Republic, Jamaica and Puerto Rico), the Virgin Islands and possibly parts of Florida, when Columbus arrived in the Caribbean in 1492. They valued the hardness, durability and, above all, the blackness of *Guaiacum* (the Latinate version of the Taino *guyacan*) for their most sacred objects. None of these was so potent as those made in human form from *Lignum vitae*. The Taino universe was an animate one in which the spirits of dead male ancestors were imbued with a life force called *cemi* or *zemi*, which

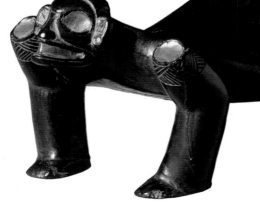

Wooden stool or *duho*, made of *Guaiacum officinale*. 15th century. L. 44 cm.

The *duho* or seat of power was used by chiefs and shamans to intercede with male ancestor spirits. Hammered gold inlay was placed in the eyes to indicate the ability to 'see' in the supernatural realm. This piece was supposedly found in a cave in Santo Domingo (the Dominican Republic), later making its way into the possession of W.O. Oldman, a London dealer and collector of ethnographic material in the first half of the twentieth century.

could assume many forms, visible and invisible. Black represented night and was equated with the absence of colour in the invisible spirit realm. The Taino appear to have hidden their sacred objects in caves, where the pieces illustrated here were found, quite possibly to preserve them from the elements and from the unwelcome attention of foreign invaders. The objects may have survived in some cases, but the Taino themselves were decimated by European disease – principally smallpox – and the wood they prized so greatly is now listed in the Convention on International Trade in Endangered Species of Wild Fauna and Flora (CITES).

Laurus nobilis

THE NYMPH Daphne, whose name means 'laurel', is the subject of one of the best known of Ovid's *Metamorphoses*:

"Her prayer was scarcely ended when a deep languor took hold on her limbs, her soft breast was enclosed in thin bark, her hair grew into leaves, her arms into branches, and her feet that were lately so swift were held fast by sluggish roots, while her face became the treetop . . . Even as a tree, Phoebus loved her . . . Since you cannot be my bride, surely you will at least be my tree. My hair, my lyre, my quivers will always display the laurel. You will accompany the generals of Rome, when the Capitol beholds their long triumphal processions, when joyful voices raise the song of victory. You will stand by Augustus's gateposts too, faithfully guarding his doors, and keeping watch from either side over the wreath of oak leaves that will hang there. Further, as my head is ever young, my tresses never shorn, so do you also, at all times, wear the crowning glory of never-fading foliage."[1]

Daphne's transformation into a bay laurel tree is wonderfully captured in a dish made for one of the most celebrated of all Renaissance dinner services, commissioned in 1524 by Eleanora d'Este for her mother Isabella d'Este, Marchioness of Mantua. The bay laurel, *Laurus nobilis*, also known as sweet bay, bay tree, true laurel and Grecian laurel, is an aromatic evergreen tree with green, glossy leaves, native to the Mediterranean region. It was used to fashion the wreaths of ancient Greece, given as a prize at the Pythian Games held at Delphi in honour of Phoebus/Apollo. This symbolism was adopted by the Romans, for whom the tree held another special significance after an eagle dropped a laurel branch into the lap of Livia Drusilla (58 BC–AD 29), following her betrothal to Augustus, first emperor of Rome:

RAPHAEL PINXIT IN VATICANO

OPPOSITE
Nicola da Urbino (*c.* 1480–1537/8), tin-glazed earthenware bowl showing scenes from Ovid: Apollo and the Python, Cupid and Apollo, and Apollo chasing Daphne, with the arms of the Gonzaga. 1524. Diam. 27.1 cm.

Daphne, on the far right of the scene, is at the very moment of metamorphosis as Phoebus/Apollo closes upon her and her father, the river god Peneus (shown below), effects her release from her captivating beauty. The imagery is taken from a woodcut illustrating a masterpiece of early printing in Venice, *Ovidio metamorphoseos vulgare* of 1497.

ABOVE
Marcantonio (1470/82–1527/34), Apollo on Parnassus. 1510–20. Engraving, 35.8 x 47 cm.

Apollo is surrounded by laurel trees, in the company of the nine Muses, and poets both ancient and modern. It is related to an early design by Raphael for his fresco of 1511 in the Stanze della Segnatura (Room of the Signature) in the Vatican in Rome.

So the augurs ordered that the bird and any chickens it produced should be preserved, and that the branch should be planted in the ground and guarded with religious care. This was done at the country mansion of the Caesars . . . the laurel grove, so begun, has thriven in a marvellous way. Afterwards the Emperor, when going in triumph, held a laurel branch from the original tree in his hand and wore a wreath of its foliage on his head and subsequently everyone of the ruling Caesars did the same.[2]

Pliny referred to the laurel as being alone among 'the shrubs planted by man and received into our houses' in never having been struck by lightning. This miraculous property inspired the 'Dangers averted' medal, associated with Elizabeth I of England who, like the bay tree, had survived unscathed the 'storm' of the Armada in 1588.

Laurisilva forests made up of laurel-leaved evergreen hardwood trees from several different genera, including *Laurus*, once covered many of the islands in the eastern Atlantic – Madeira, the Azores, western Canary islands and Cape Verde among them – and the north-west African mainland. Because they have been so greatly depleted, the largest stands that remain on Madeira were designated as a UNESCO World Heritage site in 1999.

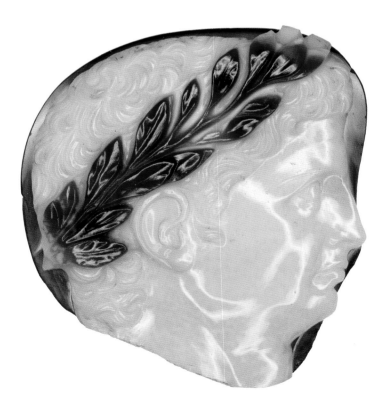

ABOVE
Nicholas Hilliard (*c.* 1547–*c.* 1619), 'Dangers Averted': chased and cast gold medal celebrating the defeat of the Spanish Armada, labelled 'E[lizabeth] R[egina]'. *c.* 1589. Diam. 4.4 cm.

On the reverse a bay tree is shown on an island, unharmed by lightning and tempest, and accompanied by the legend (in Latin), 'Not even danger affects it'.

LEFT
Sardonyx cameo with a head of the emperor Claudius (reigned AD 41–54) wearing a laurel wreath. AD 41–50. H. 6.2 cm.

OPPOSITE
Stone mosaic of a laurel wreath, with Greek inscription. From Halicarnassus (Bodrum), Turkey. 4th century AD. 114 x 114 cm.

The discovery of this mosaic in December 1856 in a field 'belonging to an old Turk called Hadji Captan' was described by Sir Charles Newton, later Keeper of Classical Antiquities at the British Museum. The Greek inscription within the wreath – 'Health, Life, Joy, Peace, Cheerfulness, Hope' – he called 'a very pleasant inscription for the eyes of the ancient owner of this villa to rest on as he paced up and down this corridor'. (*Travels and Discoveries of the Levant*, II, London 1865, vol. 2, p. 80).

Malus

ONE OF the most widely cultivated of fruits and the most suggestive of symbols, the apple is a literary and visual motif that appears throughout Western culture, from the Garden of the Hesperides, the Judgement of Paris and the Fall of Man to Snow White, New York City, the Beatles' record label and a multinational consumer electronics company. Its associations range from erotic love and fatal attraction to rude health, wholesome happiness and the bounty of nature. Mankind has played an equal role to nature in the creation of *Malus pumila Mill*; a history of domestication over many millennia has resulted in more than 7,500 cultivars across the world, all of which share a common ancestry – as shown by recent DNA sequencing – with *Malus sieversii*, a wild apple native to the Tien Shan Mountains that border China and Kazakhstan. Apples are significant to both these countries: Almaty, the capital of Kazakhstan, was formerly known as Alma-Ata ('father of apples' or 'where the apples are'), and China is today the world's biggest exporter of apples.

RIGHT
Edith Dawson (1862–1928), *Siberian Crab Apples,* *c.* 1910–13. Colour woodcut, 14.8 x 19.6 cm.

The Siberian crab apple (*Malus baccata*) is native to most of Asia. Edith Dawson, together with her husband, was an enameller and decorative designer of the Arts and Crafts movement.

OPPOSITE, LEFT
Perino del Vaga (1501–47), *Vertumnus and Pomona. c.* 1527. Red chalk, 17.6 x 13.7 cm.

This drawing, from the founding bequest of Sir Hans Sloane, was a study for one of a series of engravings on the 'Loves of the Gods', taken from Ovid. Vertumnus, who could assume different guises, has stripped off 'the trappings of age' to reveal himself 'in all his glory'. It was not Pomona's apples he wanted but the nymph herself: 'He was preparing to use force, but there was no need for that. The nymph, entranced by the god's beauty, was smitten with a passion equal to his own.' (*Metamorphoses* 767–72)

OPPOSITE, RIGHT
Walter Crane (1845–1915), earthenware vase depicting the daughters of Hesperus, painted in gold lustre on a scarlet red ground. Made at Pilkington's factory, Lancashire, 1906. H. 33.9 cm.

The beauty of the poetic image of the 'nymphs of the evening' in the paradise at the edge of the world (once thought to be where Cape Verde is, off the west coast of Africa) was vividly captured by Crane's contemporary, Frederick Lord Leighton, in his painting *The Garden of the Hesperides* of 1892.

The seeds of *Malus sieversii* were disseminated around 10,000 years ago along the network of Central Asian superhighways that later became known as the Silk Road. Apples were being cultivated in ancient Mesopotamia at least from the third millennium BC. From there they became a common orchard fruit in ancient Greece where, in Homer's *Odyssey*, the hero Odysseus was able to convince his father that he really was his son by identifying the trees Laertes had planted for him as a youth: 'You gave me thirteen pear, ten apple trees and forty figs'.[1] Alexander the Great's campaigns against the Achaemenid Empire took him as far afield as Sogdian Rock in Bactria, near Samarkand, giving his gardeners the opportunity to graft from apple trees in Central Asia, as well as closer to home in Mesopotamia and Asia Minor. The technique of grafting was quickly learned by the Romans, who propagated apple trees throughout Europe, grafting *Malus sieversii* on to the wild crab apple, *Malus sylvestris*. As well as continuing to grow in the wild, *Malus sylvestris* has also been cultivated for its decorative appearance in garden design.

The practical details of husbandry blend with mythology in Ovid's story of Vertumnus and Pomona:

It was under this king [Aventinus] that Pomona lived. No other Latin wood nymph could tend a garden more skilfully than she, none was more devoted to the cultivation of the fruit trees from which she derived her name. She did not care for woods or rivers, but loved the countryside and branches, loaded with luscious apples. Instead of weighing down her hands with heavy javelins, she used to carry a curved knife, luxurious, and prune back branches that were spreading in different directions, at another she would slit open the bark of a tree, and insert a cutting, supplying nourishing sap to a nursling from a different stock.[2]

The apple's fateful role in the affairs of men began in Greek mythology with Zeus's consort Hera, and the Hesperides or daughters of Hesperus, nymphs who tended her orchard in the west: 'Th' Hesperian maids, who watch, beyond the verge of sounding ocean, apples fair of gold, Trees bearing golden fruitage.'[3] As further insurance against theft Hera installed a dragon or serpent in the garden, but Herakles succeeded in bearing off the golden apples as his eleventh Labour. No matter that the prize may well have been citrus fruit, the apple was quickly established as the object in question. The fruit appeared again at the wedding of Peleus and Thetis, later the parents of Achilles. As revenge for her exclusion Eris, the goddess of strife, cast a golden apple addressed to the fairest of the goddesses, to which Aphrodite, Athena and Hera each laid claim. Zeus delegated the decision to Paris, the shepherd prince, who bestowed the golden apple on Aphrodite after she had promised him the love of the most beautiful woman in the world, Helen of Sparta, wife of the Greek king Menelaus; and thus the scene was set for the Trojan War.

The other notorious apple of discord is the fruit of the tree of the knowledge of good and evil in the Garden of Eden. This had an equally tenuous basis for its subsequent identification, since the fruit is not named in the biblical account. But the apple soon asserted its ascendancy in the iconographic tradition and the temptation of Eve by the serpent – the cause of original sin – became one of the most erotically charged images in Western art.

The Renaissance saw a burgeoning interest in the cultivation and representation of plants for economic, scientific and aesthetic reasons. Pomology, the study of fruit

Bronze figure of Herakles at the tree of the Hesperides.
1st century AD. H. 104.5 cm.

This sculpture came from Byblos, the Phoenician port used for shipping the cedars of Lebanon (see p. 78), which was under Roman rule from 64 BC to AD 395. It was part of the collection of Roman sculpture formed by Charles Towneley (1737–1805), purchased by the British Museum in 1805.

ABOVE
Gilt-copper watch-case with painted
enamel decoration, depicting the
Judgement of Paris. Movement made
by Lenhart Engelschalk in Friedberg,
Bavaria, 1650–60. Diam. 5 cm.

The back of this watch-case shows
the abduction of Helen of Troy,
one of the consequences of the
Judgement of Paris. There is written
evidence for the existence of watches
from the early sixteenth century in
southern Germany, where Friedberg
became a centre of production.

LEFT
Albrecht Dürer (1471–1528),
Adam and Eve. 1504. Engraving,
25 x 19.2 cm.

Dürer made several preparatory
drawings for this engraving, of which
there are two in the British Museum.
The figure of Eve was of particular
interest to him, representing the
culmination of his study of human
proportion.

production and the ways of selecting the varieties best suited for particular regions and purposes, developed as a branch of agriculture and science from the latter part of the seventeenth century onwards. The 'pome' fruits are principally apples, pears, medlars and quinces, as distinct from the stone fruits such as peach, plum, apricot and cherry (see *Prunus*, p. 146). Although most apples were cultivated for eating, others were grown specifically for cider-making, which was an important industry in many parts of Europe and a taxable commodity. Together with his book on forest trees, *Sylva* (see p. 19), in 1664 John Evelyn published *Pomona or An Appendix concerning Fruit-Trees in relation to Cider, the Making and several ways of Ordering it*.

The late eighteenth and nineteenth centuries were the heyday for the dissemination of new types of apples and pears. Pomological cabinets were formed, such as the one at the Naturkunde Museum in Bamberg, with wooden and wax models for the better study of the fruit and the demonstration of the different characteristics of the various strains. Horticultural and pomological societies encouraged competition to produce new varieties. The apple tree was introduced by early colonists to America, and that country was exporting the fruit back to England by the early nineteenth century, when in 1821–2 William Cobbett imported the seeds of Newtown Pippins for his four-acre seed and tree farm at Kensington.

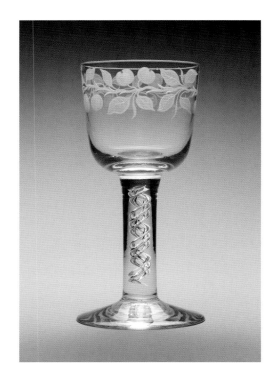

Myles Birket Foster (1825–99), An apple tree. 1860s.
Watercolour over graphite, 20.1 x 25.9 cm.

Many of Birket Foster's idyllic scenes of English rural
life were inspired by the Surrey countryside, where he
settled in 1863.

The American writer Henry Thoreau (see p. 18) summed up the relationship between mankind and the apple in one of the last pieces he completed, *Wild Apples*, written for the journal *The Atlantic Monthly* in 1862. Although its main purpose was to extol the special qualities of the crab apple (*Malus sylvestris*), he began with a short general history of the apple:

It is as harmless as a dove, as beautiful as a rose, and as valuable as flocks and herds. It has been longer cultivated than any other, and so is more humanized; and who knows but, like the wild dog, it will at length be no longer traceable to its wild original? [in this Thoreau was wrong, of course]. It migrates with man, like the dog and horse and cow: first perchance from Greece to Italy, thence to England, thence to America; and our Western emigrant is still marching steadily toward the setting sun with the seeds of the apple in his pocket, or perhaps a few young trees strapped to his load. At least a million apple-trees are thus set farther westward this year than any cultivated ones grew last year. Consider how the Blossom-Week, like the Sabbath, is thus annually spreading over the prairies; for when man migrates, he carries with him not only his birds, quadrupeds, insects, vegetables, and his very sward, but his orchard also.

Vincent van Gogh (1853–90), *Gardener by an apple tree*. 1883. Lithograph, 25 x 32.5 cm.

The composition arose from sketches made in the grounds of a Dutch Reformed House for the Elderly in The Hague, whose residents or 'orphan men and women' were often used as models by Van Gogh. He experimented with lithography while he was living in The Hague from 1882 to 1883, hoping to use it to get his work better known through publication in journals. His articulation of the leafless apple tree invites comparison with the Japanese prints by artists such as Hiroshige (p. 148) that came to his attention in the 1880s.

Morus

THE MOST commonly encountered species of mulberry are *Morus rubra* (red mulberry), *Morus nigra* (black mulberry) and *Morus alba* (white mulberry), the first two being distinguished by the succulence of their fruit. Native to eastern North America, *Morus rubra* is now present in other parts of the world. *Morus nigra*, which originated in south-west Asia, was a great favourite with the Romans for the wine and syrup that could be made from its fruit, as well as for the fruit itself. Pliny remarked that 'It is in this tree that human ingenuity has effected the least improvement of them all; there are no varieties here, no modifications effected by grafting, nor, in fact, any other improvement except that the size of the fruit, by careful management has been increased'.[1] In Britain its cultivation was given royal impetus in 1608 when, in response to the rising consumption of luxury goods, James I issued an edict for the planting of mulberry trees to encourage silk production; however, the plants in question proved to be of the black mulberry species rather than the white required for this purpose. One of the black mulberry trees linked to the edict of 1608 survives today at Christ's College, Cambridge. The black mulberry was also the subject of the nursery rhyme 'Here we go round the mulberry bush', thought to refer to the planting of mulberry trees in prison exercise yards (such as the one that still grows today at Wakefield Prison in Yorkshire).

The white mulberry from east Asia, on the other hand, is known chiefly as the sole source of food for the larvae or caterpillars of *Bombyx mori*, the moth that produces the finest white silk: 104 kilograms of mulberry leaves and 3000 silkworms are required to make 1 kilogram of silk. The extraordinary properties of the silkworm made it the subject of constant wonder, including one of the first studies in microscopy, by Marcello Malpighi (1628–94), often called 'the father of microbiology'. His history of the silkworm, written in Bologna in 1668, was the basis on which he was admitted as a member of the Royal Society in London the following year.

Chinese tradition dates the discovery of the silkworm's potential to 2700 BC, but there is evidence of sericulture (the cultivation of silkworms) even earlier, around the fourth millennium BC, making it the oldest form of 'industrial' farming. From the latter half of the first millennium BC silk was being traded outside China to India, western Asia and the Mediterranean along the Central Asian routes collectively known as the Silk Road. The Chinese maintained their monopoly of its

ABOVE
Jade silkworm. China, Zhou dynasty, *c.* 1100–901 BC. L. 5 cm.

RIGHT
Pair of silk fragments, probably a headpiece for a banner, found in Cave 17, Dunhuang, China, 3rd–5th century AD. 20.5 x 15.8 cm.

These fragments were found in the same cave as the later painting of the Buddha preaching beneath a jewelled Bodhi tree (see p. 102).

OPPOSITE
Jacobus van Huysum (1687/9–1740), White mulberry. After 1723. Watercolour over graphite, 37.5 x 26.5 cm.

From an album of plants whose names were registered by the Society of Gardeners at monthly meetings held at Chelsea in London (see p. 16).

125

Kitao Shigemasa (1739–1820), Picking mulberry leaves, from a series of ten prints about silk production. Late 18th century. Woodblock print, 23.5 x 17.8 cm.

Trades and occupations were a common subject for Chinese and Japanese woodblock printing, with sericulture prominent among them.

BELOW
Painted wooden votive panel depicting the Silk Princess. From Dandan-Uiliq (The Place of Houses of Ivory), Khotan, 7th–8th century AD. 12 x 46 cm.

production for another thousand years; thereafter the secret of its manufacture spread to Khotan, Korea, Japan and India, reaching the Byzantine Empire in the sixth century AD.

Something so exotic and shrouded in mystery inevitably created its own mythology. There are many stories as to how the secret of silk travelled beyond China. Khotan in Central Asia was the first place to practise sericulture outside China. Frustrated by the Chinese refusal to part with the essential information and ingredients, the king of Khotan sought the hand of an imperial princess, telling her that if she wanted to continue to wear silk when she was married, she would have to bring the means for its production to Khotan. This she did, concealing the seeds of the mulberry tree and the eggs of the silkworm in her headdress to avoid detection by Chinese border officials. The legend is captured on a wooden votive panel from a Buddhist shrine in Khotan, discovered at the beginning of the twentieth century on the first of three archaeological expeditions to Central Asia by the Hungarian scholar Aurel Stein (1862–1943). The panel's central figure is the Chinese princess, with an attendant pointing at her headdress; the cocoons of the silkworms are in a basket before her; at the far right another figure stands beside a loom, while the four-armed deity behind, holding a weaver's comb and shuttle, is probably the God of Silk.

The story of the introduction of silkmaking to the Byzantine Empire rests on a single account. It tells that, in AD 552, the Emperor Justinian commanded two Nestorian monks from the Christian church in Persia, who were carrying out missionary work along the Silk Road, to bring back the secret of silk from Central Asia. They smuggled silkworm eggs, which hatched en route to Constantinople, cocooning obligingly on arrival. Sericulture was spread by the Arabs around the Mediterranean, including North Africa. After the sack of Constantinople in 1204 during the Fourth Crusade, which displaced many skilled craftsmen, silk weaving became a major industry in several Italian cities, notably Lucca, but also Venice, Genoa, Florence and Milan. In 1540 the king of France, François I, granted a monopoly on silk production to the city of Lyons, which dominated the European silk trade for the next 150 years. As in east Asia, women played an important part in the cultivation of the silkworms, which was very much a domestic industry.

5. *Tum fronde, ramo, fafcibufq; conditus,*   *Se voluit, et pilæ in modum fe contrahit.*

Religious persecution in the sixteenth and seventeenth centuries brought waves of Flemish and French craftsmen to England, among them silk weavers, who congregated in Norwich in East Anglia and Spitalfields in the East End of London. The latter, in particular, began to challenge the ascendancy of Lyons. The domestic scale of the weavers' workshops was subjected to increasing competition from the silk mills that were established from the mid-eighteenth century, principally in Congleton, Derby, Macclesfield and Stockport. However, an epidemic of silkworm diseases from 1845 seriously affected the supply of silk in Europe, while competition from other fibres, especially artificial ones in the twentieth century, depressed the market. First Japan and then China regained their supremacy after the Second World War. China is now the biggest producer in the world, seconded by India which, as well as silk made from *Bombyx mori*, produces 'wild silk' made from different species of silkworm which feed not on mulberry leaves but on those of other trees.

After Jan van der Straet (1523–1605), The gathering of mulberry leaves and the feeding of the silkworms, plate 5 from the second edition of *Vermis sericus*, a series of six prints illustrating the history and techniques of silk production in Europe, engraved by Theodor Galle (1571–1633) and published by Philips Galle (1537–1612) in Antwerp. *c*. 1590–1600. 20.1 x 26.4 cm.

The title-page to the series carries a dedication to Costanza Alamanni, wife of Raffaele de' Medici (1543–1629), a member of the ruling family in Tuscany. Ferdinando de' Medici, who was Grand Duke from 1587 to 1609, oversaw the planting of mulberry trees along the major roads to augment the silk industry. Jan van der Straet from Antwerp, generally known as Stradanus, was a designer of prints and tapestries, working for much of his life in Florence, where he died in 1605. This edition of *Vermis sericus* belonged to Sir Hans Sloane.

RIGHT
After a drawing by Isaac
Cruikshank (1764–1811), *The
mulberry-tree*: heading to a printed
songsheet, published by Laurie
& Whittle, London. 1808. Hand-
coloured etching with letterpress,
28.7 x 29 cm (sheet).

In the verses printed below the
image, the mulberry tree is hailed
as being resistant to the 'dew'
(meaning mildew, which blights
other trees) and as a metaphor
for aspects of human life. The
song ends with: 'Yet like lignum
vitae we hearts of oak wear/Or
the cedar that keeps from the
cankerworm free;/While the vine-
juice we drain to dissolve ev'ry
care/Like the dew that flies over
the mulberry-tree.'

OPPOSITE
The Garrick casket, carved from
'Shakespeare's mulberry tree'
(*Morus nigra*). *c.* 1769. 21.8 x 14 cm.

The casket was presented to the
actor David Garrick (1717–79)
when he was given the freedom
of the borough of Stratford-
upon-Avon in 1769 at the time of
his Shakespeare Jubilee. There
was no evidence to connect the
tree with Shakespeare himself,
but it had become a focus for
'pilgrims' by the time the owner
of Shakespeare's former property
at New Place cut it down in 1759.
The casket, the most splendid
of many souvenirs purporting to
come from the tree, was acquired
in 1835 by George Daniel, a writer
and collector of Shakespeare first
folios, who bequeathed it to the
British Museum.

THE MULBERRY-TREE.

William Faithorne (*c.* 1620–91), illustration to *Parallelum Olivae* by Louis le Gand 'Seigneur de Brochey et de Romecour', London 1656. Engraving, 24.1 x 15.9 cm.

Le Gand had been the author of a similarly flattering work in 1641 in praise of Charles I, who was characterized as the sun or a sunflower. The engraver Faithorne was imprisoned in 1645 after serving on the Royalist side in the English Civil War. His sentence was commuted to exile in France until 1652, when he was able to resume his career in London.

130

*Archontas summos inter fœlicis OLIVÆ,
Primus OLIVARI nomen et omen habes.*

G. Faithorne fec:

MANY of the classical references to the symbolic importance of the olive were detailed in a work of slavish flattery directed at Oliver Cromwell while he was Lord Protector of the Commonwealth from 1653 to 1658. The principal illustration after the frontispiece is a 'hieroglyphic' image to be deciphered, of the kind with which the seventeenth century reader would have been familiar. The olive, or Oliver, provides the root system and stem from which all virtues grow, with Cromwell as the latter-day heir to the heroes of ancient Greece and Rome.

This is one testimony to the status of the olive, but more powerful still is the evidence of its economic worth in the ancient world. Monte Testaccio in Rome is made up of the fragments of 53 million broken amphora; these once held six billion litres of olive oil, the consumption of which is estimated to have reached its peak at the end of the second century AD. The olive was not introduced to Italy until around the fourth century BC, long after its cultivation was underway elsewhere: the earliest evidence comes from Jordan (fifth millennium BC), Minoan Crete (fourth millennium BC) and Syria (third millennium BC). Hesiod and Homer, whose narratives date to the eighth century BC, mention the cultivation of the olive tree in Greece and the islands of the archipelago. It was the first tree encountered by Odysseus when he finally made his way back to Ithaca: 'at last . . . At the harbour's head a branching olive stands with a welcome cave nearby it, dank with sea-mist, sacred to nymphs of the springs we call the Naiads'.[1] The olive was the tree sacred to Athena, Odysseus's protecting deity. Athens was built where she struck her spear into the earth and forthwith it turned into an olive tree. At the Panathenaic Games held in Athens every four years in her honour, great quantities of olive oil were presented as prizes: this would be used for heating, lighting, cooking, cleansing and lubricating the body. *Olea oleaster*, the wild olive, which ancient Greeks distinguished from the cultivated one (*Olea europaea*), was used to fashion the wreaths awarded to victors at the Olympic Games. Herakles, whose club was made from a limb of a wild olive tree, was said to have planted the sacred olive at Olympia, which was situated to the rear of the Temple of Zeus.

Early evidence of the distinction accorded to the olive outside Greece comes from a wreath of folded olive leaves preserved in the Herbarium at Kew, one of the funerary garlands found in 1924 in the sarcophagus of Tutankhamun, who died in 1327 BC.

Attributed to the Antimenes Painter (530–510 BC), black-figured pottery amphora showing olive-gathering, with Pholos receiving Herakles on the other side. Made in Athens, 520 BC. H. 40.6 cm.

The amphora was acquired in 1837 at the sale of the collection of Lucien Bonaparte, Napoleon's younger brother.

Glass vessel stamp. AD 720–34. W. 3.4 cm.

By the time Pliny was writing his *Natural History* in the first century AD, the olive had spread westwards from the Levant to North Africa, Italy, Spain and Gaul (France). The olive groves in Baetica, south-west Spain, supplied a large proportion of Rome's requirements, and were the source of wealth for the land-owning elite from which the future emperor Hadrian came (ruled AD 117–38). Spain dominates the production of olive oil today, followed by Italy and Greece. Pliny devoted a whole book to every aspect of olive cultivation, including the best method of gathering the harvest:

A third mistake is in over-economy, as owing to the cost of picking people wait for the olives to fall. Those who compromise on a middle course in this matter knock the fruit down with poles, so injuring the trees and causing loss in the following year; in fact there was a very old regulation for the olive harvest: "Neither strip nor beat an olive-tree." . . . The majesty of Rome has accorded the olive-tree great

The Biel Throne: marble throne from the Panathenaic Stadium of Herodes Attikos in Athens, AD 140–43. H. 700 cm.

honour by crowning our cavalry squadrons with wreaths of olive on the Ides of July and also when celebrating minor triumphs. Athens also crowns its victors at Olympia with wreaths of wild olive.[2]

Pliny wrote disapprovingly of the Greeks' diversion of the use of olive oil 'to serve the purpose of luxury by making it a regular practice in their gymnasiums; the governors of these institutions have been known to sell the scrapings of the oil off bodies for 80,000 sesterces'.[3] Oiling the body was particularly important for Greek athletes, who competed naked, but the practice was also common among those in the Roman world, as shown by the surviving bronze toilet sets, comprising an aryballos (oil flask) and strigils for scraping.

The most universal of all the olive's meanings is that of peace and reconciliation. This stems from the account in the Book of Genesis of the return of the dove to Noah's

Accipe iam demum vectricem Numinis Arcam,
Portus, & aeternis obrue delicijs.

✠✠✠

Apres cent tourbillons l'Arche espera le calme,
Quand elle vit briller le rameau de la paix :
La Vierge, que l'amour acable sous son faix,
Attend la liberté, quand elle voit la palme.

Jacques Callot (1592–1635), Noah's Ark, from *Vitae Beatae Mariae* (Life of the Blessed Virgin). 1625–9. 6.1 x 8.2 cm (image).

One of twenty-seven emblematic plates with text linking the images to the virtues of the Virgin, published in booklet form in 1627–8.

Bronze athlete's toilet set with an aryballos (oil-flask) and two strigils, linked by chains for hanging on a wall. Roman, 1st–2nd century AD, found in the Rhineland. L. 27 and 22 cm (strigils); H. 9.5 cm (aryballos).

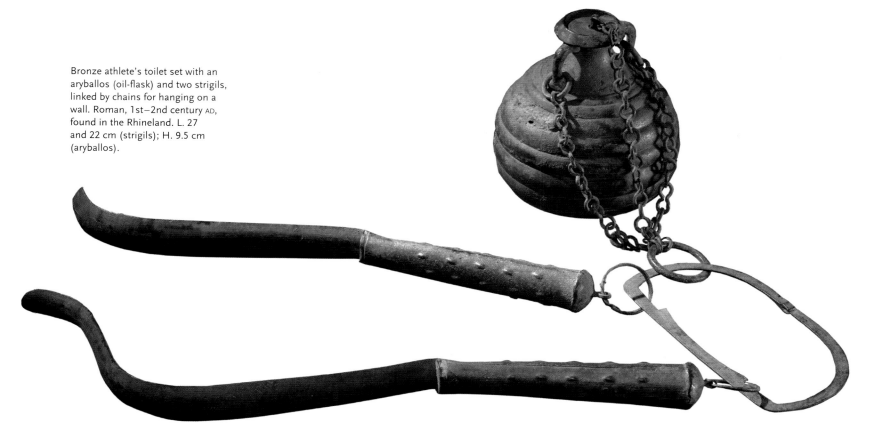

Wooden model of the Church of the Nativity in Bethlehem,
made of olive wood inlaid with mother-of-pearl and ivory.
17th –18th century. H. 17.5 cm.

Models such as this and, more commonly, of the Church of the
Holy Sepulchre in Jerusalem started to appear from the early
seventeenth century, doubtless intended as superior souvenirs and
gifts for wealthy visitors and foreign dignitaries. They were made
in Bethlehem by Palestinian craftsmen under the supervision of
the Franciscans, to whose care the Holy Land had been committed
by Pope Clement VI in 1342. This particular model appears in Sir
Hans Sloane's catalogue of his collection along with a reference to
a model of the Church of the Holy Sepulchre.

Claude Lorrain (1600–1682), Landscape with Apulian shepherd changed into an olive tree. *c.* 1657–82. Pen and brown ink with brown wash, heightened with white, 19.7 x 26 cm.

This drawing comes from the *Liber Veritatis* (Book of Truth) in the British Museum, which Claude compiled as a record of his paintings between 1635 and 1682 to guard against imitations. The subject was taken from Ovid's *Metamorphoses* where the Apulian shepherd is punished for coarsely mocking a group of dancing nymphs: 'Nothing silenced him, till finally a tree trunk imprisoned his throat: for he became a wild olive, in the taste of whose fruit one can still recognize the character of the man. In its bitter berries the tree reveals traces of his tongue, and the harshness of his language has passed into the olives.' (XIV, 519–529).

Ark, bearing an olive twig as a sign that the waters of the Flood were receding and God's wrath was abating. The tree's association with peace rather than victory existed in Greek mythology as it was an attribute of Eirene, one of the *Horae* (Hours or Seasons), who became the personification of peace. It also accompanied an aspect of the Roman god of war Mars, in the form of *Mars Pacifer*, the bringer of peace. But it was early Christian iconography that developed the symbolism combining the Flood story with the New Testament association of the dove with the Holy Spirit and baptism. The triple meaning of hope, salvation and peace bound up in this simple, affecting image has endured, becoming a secular symbol as much as a religious one.

135

Pinus

LIKE OTHER conifers, the pine has a history extending back around 300 million years. There are some 115 species of pine, rejoicing in a great variety of common names: bristle cone pine (*Pinus longaeva*), Chinese red pine (*Pinus tabuliformis*), eastern white pine or Weymouth pine (*Pinus strobus*), European black pine (*Pinus nigra*), Jack pine (*Pinus banksiana*), Italian stone or umbrella pine (*Pinus pinea*, the source of pine nuts for pesto), lacebark pine (*Pinus bungeana*), loblolly pine (*Pinus taeda*), maritime pine (*Pinus pinaster*) and Scots pine (*Pinus sylvestris*). These evergreen resinous trees grow well on poor, often acidic, sandy soils – such as those around Dürer's native Nuremberg in southern Germany – and are widely distributed throughout temperate regions. Their fossil ancestry links them to one of the genera of trees whose resin produced Baltic amber, and the living species are among the most commercially important trees for timber and wood pulp. Mathematically, pine cones are interesting because they grow in two opposing spirals of 5 and 8, adjacent numbers in the Fibonacci sequence, which was introduced to Europe from Arab sources by Leonardo Pisano (otherwise known as Fibonacci; *c.* 1170–*c.* 1250). The occurrence of the sequence in natural forms was first observed in the latter part of the nineteenth century.

In Greek poetry Pitys ('pine') was a nymph loved by Pan. Fleeing his advances, she was turned by the gods into a pine tree, probably *Pinus halepensis* (Aleppo pine), *Pinus brutia* (Turkish pine) or *Pinus nigra* (European black pine). The same fate befell the shepherd Attis, who was resurrected in this form by his lover Cybele, mother of the earth and the gods. The tree was then her favourite but, as told in Virgil's *Aeneid*, she sacrificed it to the needs of the Trojan fleet, urgently beseeching Jove to grant the ships his protection:

Once I had a wood of pines which I loved for many years . . . But when the young Dardan [Aeneas] had need of a fleet, I gladly gave my trees to him. Now however I am distressed by anxiety and fear. Dispel my alarm and allow your mother's prayers to have such

Edward Calvert (1799–1883), Pan and Pitys. 1850. Oil on paper, 19.9 x 36.3 cm.

The nymph, standing beside a pine, looks back over her shoulder at Pan, who sits secluded among the trees.

LEFT
Carved amber tankard with silver-gilt mounts. 1640–60. H. 20.5 cm.

This tankard, which may have belonged to Queen Christina of Sweden (reigned 1632–54), is carved with emblematic figures of the seven deadly sins: Pride, Gluttony, Lechery, Anger, Envy, Avarice and Sloth, and bears the coat of arms of the Swedish Royal House of Vasa (1521–1654). It is likely to have been made in Königsberg (Kaliningrad), the heart of the amber trade on the Baltic which was controlled by the Teutonic Knights from the mid-thirteenth until the sixteenth centuries, when Königsberg became part of the Duchy of Prussia. The mine at Kaliningrad still holds 90 per cent of the world's amber.

force that those ships may never be overcome, shattered by any voyage or any violence of the wind. Let it profit them that it was in my mountains that they had their origin.[1]

Naval demands have stripped many habitats of their timber. The potential in this respect of the eastern white pine or Weymouth pine (*Pinus strobus*), native to north-eastern America, was spotted by Captain George Weymouth, who brought seeds back to England in 1605. A century later the unrelated Lord Weymouth planted the seeds for ornamental purposes on his estate at Longleat, but the species found it hard to thrive in England. However, it flourished along the eastern seaboard of America, and in the 1750s the British Government decreed a pre-emptive right to the finest trees there. Pine provided not only timber for ships but also the means of caulking (sealing) and coating, to make them waterproof. By 1725 four fifths of the pitch and tar used in England came from the American colonies.

The significance of pine in North America went way beyond its economic value. The eastern white pine was the Tree of Peace, symbol of the Iroquois Confederacy

Albrecht Dürer (1471–1528), Landscape with a woodland pool. *c.* 1496. Watercolour and bodycolour, 26.2 x 36.5 cm.

This study of pine trees and water on the outskirts of Nuremberg came from the collection of Sir Hans Sloane, who acquired it in Holland in 1724 among five albums of Dürer's work. The drawings have remained with the British Museum while the manuscript material and sketches are part of the British Library's collection.

comprising the five nations of the Mohawk, Oneida, Onondaga, Cayuga and Seneca, which were joined by the Tuscarora after 1722. The Tree served to shelter all nations that committed themselves to the Great Law of Peace by burying beneath it their war hatchets and other weapons. The Iroquois Confederacy and the Great Law of Peace became an important part of the rhetoric of the American patriots in anticipation of the Declaration of Independence in 1776, and later in the framing of the United States Constitution.

In China, Japan and Korea species such as *Pinus armandii* (Chinese white pine), *Pinus densiflora* (Japanese red pine), *Pinus hwangshanensis* (Huangshan pine), *Pinus koraiensis* (Korean pine), *Pinus parviflora* (Japanese white pine), *Pinus sibirica* (Siberian pine) and *Pinus tabuliformis* (Chinese red pine) have long populated the mountain landscapes. In his 1690–92 account of Japan, Engelbert Kaempfer described how, 'the most common trees of the forest are pine and cypress of many varieties . . . These trees are planted as decoration in long rows on the top of mountain ridges and also on both sides of the highways. Great effort is made to have them grow in all sandy and uninhabited places. No pine or cypress tree may be cut without permission of the local authority, and a new sapling must be planted to replace it.'

The First Emperor of China, Qin Shi Huangdi (reigned 247–221 BC), marked the consolidation of authority along the eastern border of his empire through a series of *feng shan* rituals addressed to heaven, and the erection of commemorative stelae. Descending from Mount Tai, the most important of the Five Sacred Mountains of Daoism (sacred because they are where the powers of heaven meet earth), he had to take shelter from wind and rain under a pine tree; in gratitude this was granted the status of a fifth-rank grandee. Some of the most celebrated pines grow at Huangshan or Yellow Mountain, now a UNESCO World Heritage site, including the Ying Ke pine or Welcoming-Guests pine, thought to be more than 1500 years old.

138

Silver 'pine tree' shilling. Massachusetts, dated 1652 but issued 1667–1674 . Diam. 1.5 cm.

Currency was in short supply in the North American colonies. To counteract this, the Massachusetts colonists issued their own coins for thirty years from 1652.

BELOW
Wampum garters, made of porcupine quill woven with glass beads and wool ties. Northeast Woodlands peoples, either Iroquoian or Algonquian, 1700–1770. L. 31.5 cm.

The repeat design is that of the 'Tree of Peace' and the glass beads are in imitation of real wampum made from the shells of clams and whelks. Belts and garters were important articles of exchange, used for treaty negotiations between the Iroquois Confederacy and their European allies in the seventeenth and eighteenth centuries. The garters came from the studio of the Pennsylvania-born painter Benjamin West (1738–1820) who settled in London in 1763. He used authentic accessories for the native American figures in two of his modern history pieces of 1770 and 1771: *The Death of General Wolfe* (with reference to Wolfe's death at Quebec in 1759), and *William Penn's Treaty with the Indians* [1682].

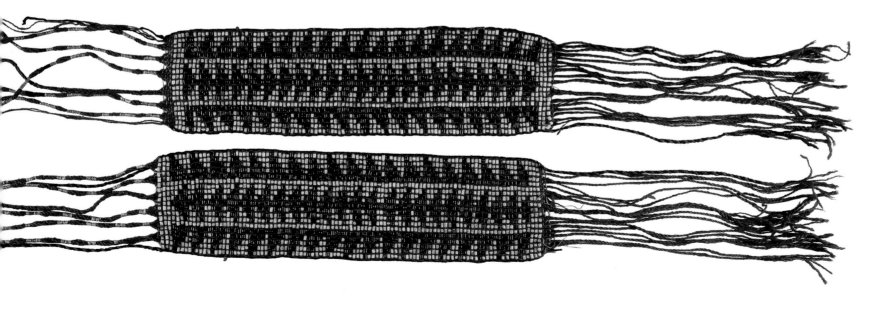

ABOVE
Utagawa Hiroshige (1797–1858),
Landscape at Mount Kano in Kazusa
province, with pilgrims climbing steps
to Jinyaji Temple and Shiratori Shrine
through pines and cypresses. 1848–58.
Ink and colour on silk, 44.7 x 60.5 cm.

RIGHT
Takamakie lacquered wood inrō showing Qin Shi Huangdi
(the First Emperor of China) conferring an honour on pine trees.
Japan, 19th century. H. 7 cm.

An inrō is a case of nested compartments for holding seals or
medicines that Japanese men would hang from the waist. By
the eighteenth century these had become significant decorative
accessories on which great skill and artistry were expended.
'Takamakie' is a technique of building up the surface using
metallic powder and lacquer pigments.

Pines are symbols of longevity, steadfastness and survival in adversity because they
can withstand the cold; they are often shown with cranes, another symbol of longevity
(see the ink painting overleaf). Together with bamboo and *Prunus* (see p. 146), the pine
is one of the 'Three Friends of Winter', so called because they bloom early in the year
(in the case of the plum), or remain green throughout. In the ballad *The Source of the Peach
Blossom Stream* by the Tang dynasty poet Wang Wei (701–761), the pines are part of the
otherworldliness of the hidden enclave in the mountains, where the fisherman is
led by the stream, a place 'where clouds and trees converged':

The people that lived there dressed
in a style
unaltered since the Qin . . .
Tending their fields and gardens still,
Beyond the world of things.
Under the pines in the bright moon
Their houses were quite still.
At first they had left the world of men
To escape from war and strife,
But then they had become immortals,
So they had not returned.[2]

The pine cone has its own special
associations. In Greek mythology it
appeared on top of the thyrsus, a staff of
giant fennel (*Ferula communis*) covered
with ivy vines, which was first carried by
Dionysus and his followers, and then as an
attribute of the Roman cult of Bacchus.
It was attached as a finial to Roman water
jets, most impressively the massive bronze
Fontana della Pigna, which was originally
located near the Pantheon next to the
Temple of Isis, and is now in the Cortile
della Pigna within the Vatican City.

The Italian composer Ottorino
Respighi (1879–1936) made the pines
of Rome (*Pinus pinea*) the subject of his
symphonic poem *Pini di Roma* (1924), part of a trilogy with *Fontane di Roma* (Fountains
of Rome, 1916) and *Feste Romane* (Roman Festivals, 1926). The four movements evoke
the glories of ancient Rome and the link between past and present, starting with a
contemporary scene of children playing a game of soldiers among the pines of the Villa
Borghese, then moving back into the past with 'Pines near a catacomb' and 'The Pines
of the Janiculum'. In the final movement, 'The Pines of the Appian Way', a Roman
legion marches at dawn along the Appian Way towards the summit of the Capitoline.

140

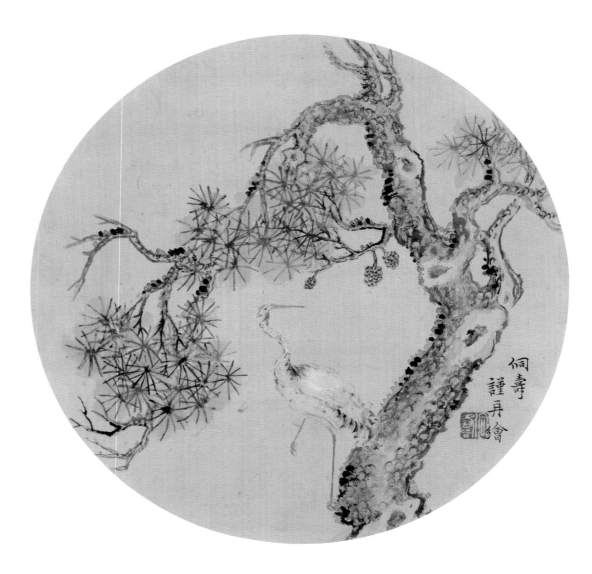

Crane and pine tree: painting for a fan from
an album. China, Qing dynasty (1644–1911), 18th
century. Ink and colours on silk, diam. 23.8 cm.

LEFT
Bronze fountain jet. Pompeii, 1st century AD.
H. 53.3 cm.

RIGHT
Edward Millington Synge (1860–1913), Study of trees,
Villa Borghese. 1903. Etching, 19.1 x 14 cm.

BELOW
Georg Dionysius Ehret (1708–70), Study of *Pinus americana
palustris. c.* 1741. Watercolour and bodycolour on vellum,
53.4 x 36.7 cm.

Ehret, born in Heidelberg, was an outstanding botanical
draughtsman with connections to all the leading naturalists
and gardeners of his day. He had met Linnaeus in Holland
before coming to England in 1736, where he worked
with Sir Hans Sloane, Philip Miller of the Chelsea Physic
Garden, Peter Collinson, the Duchess of Portland and at
the university botanical garden in Oxford. Philip Miller
inscribed this sheet, incorrectly linking *Pinus americana
palustris* to the marsh pine. The latter is *Pinus serotina* while
the former is commonly known as the longleaf pine, native
to the south-eastern United States, including Virginia.

PINUS *Americana palustris*

Populus

These stately trees, aspiring to the grace
of heaven with their upper branches starched,
line up on roadsides, measuring the march
Napoleonic troops took . . .
    Lyn Moir, 'Lombardy poplars' (2005)[1]

THE Lombardy poplar (*Populus nigra 'Italica'*) is the variety of poplar that most readily comes to a European mind familiar with the planting encouraged in France by Napoleon, having seen their value as 'sentinels', visible from afar, on his campaigns in Italy. It is a variant of the black poplar, *Populus nigra*, which originated in western Asia, and was present in seventeenth-century Persian and Mughal Indian gardens, such as the one built by the Emperor Jahangir (reigned 1605–27) at Shalimar bagh in Kashmir. The Lombardy variant arose through selective cultivation of 'fastigiate', or upright, forms in Italy in the seventeenth century. From there it was introduced to France in 1749, Britain in 1758 and North America in 1784, rapidly gaining ground as a tree for avenues and ornamental landscaping. The tree achieved renown as a romantic motif because of the stand of poplars that surrounded the tomb of the philosopher Jean-Jacques Rousseau on the Ile des Peupliers (Island of Poplars) in the park at Ermenonville, northern France. The owner of the estate and designer of the garden, the Marquis de Girardin, was an avid admirer of Rousseau, who stayed at Ermenonville on several occasions, dying there in 1778. The Island of Poplars became a place of pilgrimage for many notable figures, among them Benjamin Franklin and Thomas Jefferson, Danton, Robespierre and Napoleon.

The widespread adoption in France of the Lombardy poplar, with its striking verticality, led to its appropriation as a Liberty Tree during the French Revolution and beyond. Liberty Trees were originally an American phenomenon, hung with flags and devices and crowned with the Phrygian cap (a Roman symbol of liberty) during the War of Independence. There was no exclusivity when it came to the kind of tree chosen for this role; although 'poplars' were planted as Liberty Trees in America, they were tulip poplars, *Lirodendron tulipifera*, and not

142

OPPOSITE
François Godefroy (1743–1819), after a drawing by Gandat (Swiss landscape painter, d. 1797 in Ermenonville), *The grave of J.J. Rousseau in the garden at Ermenonville*. 1781. Etching, 52.7 x 39.3 cm.

BELOW
Jacobus van Huysum (1687/9–1740), Black poplar (*Populus nigra*). Watercolour over graphite, 37.5 x 26.5 cm.

From an album of plants whose names were registered at monthly meetings of a Society of Gardeners in London from *c.* 1723 onwards (see p. 16).

144

Michelangelo (1475–1564), The fall of Phaeton.
1531–3. Black chalk over stylus underdrawing,
31.2 x 21.5 cm.

Michelangelo conflated the moment in Ovid's
Metamorphoses (II, 294–366) when Jupiter's
thunderbolt destroys Phaeton's fiery chariot with that
of the metamorphosis of his grieving sisters into trees.
Later on Ovid referred to them as poplars when, with
other trees, they are drawn by the music of Orpheus.

of the *Populus* genus. In France, however, Lombardy poplars
were readily to hand. In his unfinished satirical novel *Bouvard
et Pécuchet*, published posthumously in 1881, Flaubert
observed – with reference to the 1848 political upheavals and
their subsequent suppression – how Liberty Trees (poplars)
were planted in revolutionary times, then cut down in
reactionary ones.

The leaves of the white poplar, *Populus alba*, are white on
one side and green on the other. Part of the genus that includes
aspens (e.g. *Populus tremula*), the species is mentioned in
classical sources as having been introduced to Greece by
Herakles, after it was consecrated to him in honour of the tenth
of his Labours. In the Roman version of the story he bound his
brow with a garland of white poplar to celebrate the slaying of
the cattle-stealing monster Cacus, who dwelt in a cave on the
Aventine Hill in Rome, which was covered with white poplars.
In Ovid's *Metamorphoses*, the Heliades or 'children of the sun'
were turned into trees – probably *Populus alba* – by the gods,
having been unwittingly complicit in the catastrophic demise of
their brother Phaeton by harnessing his horses to the chariot of the sun.

Populus sect. *Aegiros* includes three species of poplar native to Europe, western Asia
and North America. Known in America by the common name of cottonwood (*Populus
deltoides*), it achieved notoriety in the song *Strange Fruit*, first sung by Billie Holliday in
1939 to lyrics by Abel Meeropol, which evoked the shocking image of lynched African-
Americans:

> Southern trees bear a strange fruit
> Blood on the leaves and blood at the root,
> Black body swinging in the Southern breeze,
> Strange fruit hanging from the poplar trees.

C.J. Grant (fl. 1830–52), *The pop'lar tree*. June 1831.
Hand-coloured etching, 24.6 x 15.3 cm.

The poplar or 'popular' tree is an allusion to the
symbolic Tree of the Constitution and provides the
locus for a commentary on the political ferment that
led up to the Great Reform Bill of 1832. In the tree
are the 'blank' silhouettes of the king William IV at
the top, then below Lords Grey, Brougham, Russell
and Durham who were of the Whig, pro-Reform party.
Rats, i.e. the reformers, gnaw at the base of the trunk,
attempting to undermine the constitution. Below the
text reads: 'With a firm deep Root, to it's Native Soil
it clings /And despite of Storms or Vermin upward
Springs /Foster'd by Freedom's Race it Stands Alone /
Shoots Promised Fruit and hails the Rising Sun.'

Plum, Apricot, Peach and Cherry

THE GENUS *Prunus* includes several flowering trees that have long been cultivated for their fruit and for ornament, including plum, apricot, peach and cherry. These trees are held in particularly high esteem in east Asia, largely for the beauty of their flowers, but the fruit of the apricot and peach trees also carries symbolic significance.

In China the plum (*Prunus mume*, Chinese plum or Japanese apricot) is a symbol of winter and harbinger of spring, signifying perseverance and longevity because it blooms at the end of winter, before leaves appear on the trees. The five petals of its blossom make it auspicious, as they represent the Five Blessings: a long life, wealth, health, love of virtue and a peaceful death. The tree also holds significance in Chinese culture as one of the 'Three Friends of Winter' (with the pine and bamboo); one of the 'Four Gentlemen' (with the orchid, chrysanthemum and bamboo); and one of the flowers that represent the Four Seasons: orchid (spring), lotus (summer), chrysanthemum (autumn) and plum (winter). The 'Three Friends of Winter', symbolizing perseverance, integrity and modesty, first emerged as a motif in the poetry and then the painting of the tenth-century Song dynasty. They are often equated with the three religions of China – Buddhism, Daoism and Confucianism – or with the ideal qualities of the gentleman-scholar. Such traditional symbolism survived into the Communist era. Mao Zedong (1893–1976) was a keen calligrapher and poet, and used both skills to enhance his authority. In 1963 he published a collection of poems written over the preceding thirty-five years, which included *In Praise of the Winter Plum Blossom* of 9 December 1961, his response to *Ode to Plum Blossom* by the Tang dynasty poet Lu Yu (AD 733–804):

> Spring disappears with rain and winds
> And comes with flying snow.
> Ice hangs on a thousand feet of cliff
> Yet at the tip of the topmost branch the plum
> blooms.
>
> The plum is not a delicious girl showing off
> yet she heralds spring
> When mountain flowers are in wild bloom
> She giggles in all the colour.[1]

School of Qiu Ying (*c.* 1494–*c.* 1552), Hanging scroll of ladies beneath a plum tree. China, Ming dynasty (1368–1644), *c.* 1500. Ink and colours on silk with a painted ground, 102.7 x 50.7 cm.

Richard Nixon recalled the interpretation of this poem that he was given by Zhou Enlai (first Premier of the People's Republic of China) on his visit to China in 1972. Its meaning was explained thus: he who takes the initiative will not be the one to

Prunus

Three porcelain wine cups painted in enamel colours depicting, from top to bottom, *Prunus mume* (plum), *Prunus armeniaca* (apricot) and *Prunus persica* (peach). From a group of twelve cups with each month represented by a different seasonal tree, flower or shrub, China, Qing dynasty (1644–1911), 1662–1722. Each cup H. 5 cm.

These are rare survivors of a type of ceramic that was popular in the early 18th century.

Attributed to Kano School, two-panel screen showing a red plum tree and a broken bamboo stalk. Japan, early 17th century, Momoyama period (1573–1603)/ Edo period (1603–1868). Ink, colour and gold on paper, 176 x 191 cm.

Bamboo and plum are two of the 'Three Friends of Winter', the other being pine.

Utagawa Hiroshige (1797–1858), Plum Estate Kameido. 11th lunar month 1857. Colour woodblock print, 35 x 22.8 cm.

This print is no. 30 in Hiroshige's series *100 Views of Edo* (Tokyo). The tree in the foreground was given the name Resting Dragon Plum because its branches grew so long they reached the ground.

experience its fulfilment because, by the time the flowers are in full bloom, they are ready to wither and die. By the time Nixon returned to China in 1976, he was out of office and Zhou Enlai was dead.

The visual and symbolic appeal held by the flowering *Prunus* in the East was introduced to the West through Japanese decorative arts, especially prints, after the opening up of Japan to foreign trade from 1859. Hiroshige's last great series of woodblock prints, *100 Views of Edo* (1856–8), included a striking image of a plum orchard, which Van Gogh acquired and copied in oils in 1887.

Apricot (*Prunus armeniaca*) and peach (*Prunus persica*) were introduced to Europe from China via the Silk Road and Alexander the Great's military campaigns, though apricot was long believed to have originated in Armenia and peach in Persia. On a dish made for the sixtieth birthday of the Kangxi emperor (reigned 1662–1722) in 1713, the combination of three apricots and a magpie produces the auspicious message 'joyfully announcing the achievement of three firsts'; the magpie is a bird of joy and the apricots stand for first places in the provincial, metropolitan and imperial examinations for the Chinese civil service. Apricots bloom in the second lunar month, when the last of these examinations was held, and successful candidates were invited to a banquet in the Apricot Grove of the imperial garden.

Peach and plum blossom are standard decoration at the Chinese New Year, the Spring Festival when flowering saplings are grown indoors and their blossoms considered a sign of wealth and prosperity in the coming year. But the fruit is particularly important because of the association between peaches and longevity. Xi Wangmu, the Queen Mother of the West, is a Daoist figure who lives in the paradise of the Kun Lun mountains and is often depicted with the peaches of immortality that grow there. Her trees only blossom once every three thousand years, and the peaches take another three thousand years to ripen.

The Romans were cultivating apricots and peaches in the first century AD, when Pliny remarked: 'As for the peach-tree, it was only introduced lately, and that with difficulty, inasmuch as in Rhodes, which was its first place of sojourn after leaving Egypt, it does not bear at all'.[2] The trees were not recorded in England until the sixteenth century, when Henry VIII's gardener was

TOP
Famille verte enamelled porcelain dish with a magpie on a fruiting apricot branch. China, Qing dynasty (1644–1911), 1713. Diam. 14.5 cm.

LEFT
Mary Delany (1700–1788), *Prunus armeniaca*, apricot. 1779. Collage of coloured papers with bodycolour and watercolour, and with leaf sample, on black ink background, 28.6 x 22.4 cm.

Jan Bosschaert (fl. 1610/11–28), Branch of a plum
tree (*Prunus domestica* or damson plum). 1623.
Bodycolour, 20 x 31 cm.

This is from one of five albums stamped '1637' that
Sir Hans Sloane acquired in Holland in 1724. The
other four albums contained the work of Dürer.
Prunus domestica was first cultivated in Syria and
introduced to Europe by the Romans.

LEFT
Jacques Le Moyne (c. 1533–88), Peach. c. 1585.
Watercolour and bodycolour on vellum,
21.3 x 14 cm.

From the album of fifty watercolours of fruit and trees that came to light in 1961 (see p. 120).

RIGHT
Famille rose enamelled porcelain vase with peach branch and flowers. China, Qing dynasty (1644–1911), Yongzheng period (1723–35). H. 52 cm.

The nine peaches on this vase represent the highest *yang* (male principle) number, which stands for eternity.

BELOW
Stoneware water-dropper made in Yixing, China, Qing dynasty (1644–1911), 18th century. L. 16.8 cm.

This was part of the equipment of the scholar's desk for the practice of calligraphy, along with the ink stone on which the water would be dropped to mix the ink. The shape of the peach would have been regarded as particularly auspicious.

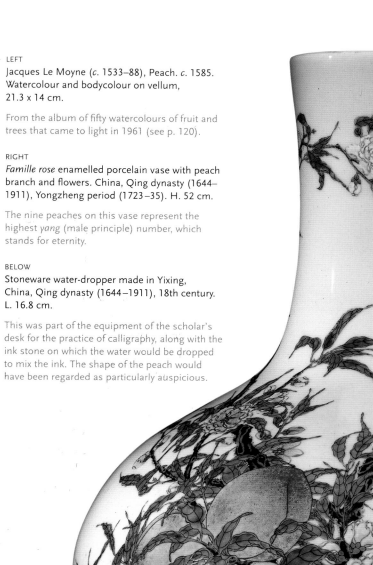

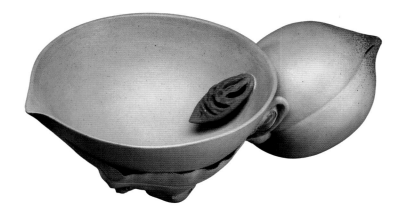

credited with bringing apricot seedlings from Italy in 1542. In *The Two Noble Kinsmen*, a collaborative work by Shakespeare and John Fletcher from 1613, one of the kinsman, Palamon, speaks enviously of an apricot tree as a means to attaining the object of his desire:

> . . . Would I were,
> For all the fortune of my life hereafter,
> Yon little tree, yon blooming apricot –
> How I would spread and fling my wanton arms
> In at her window! I would bring her fruit
> Fit for the gods to feed on.[3]

'Hanami', meaning 'to see flowers', was an ancient Japanese tradition of picnicking under a blossoming tree. This was originally the plum ('*ume*'), but by the twelfth century '*hanami*' was associated with the ornamental cherry trees now known as the Japanese cherry or *Prunus serrulata*. Its first literary mention was in 'The Festival of the Cherry Blossoms', the eighth chapter of the eleventh-century novel *The Tale of Genji*, written by a woman, Murasaki Shikibu. The custom was restricted at first to members of the Imperial Court, but later spread to other classes of society, becoming widespread during the Edo period (1603–1868). People today continue to turn out in celebration of the blooming of the cherry trees, which starts in southern Japan in January or early February, and spreads to Kyoto and Tokyo in March and April.

In his account of Japan from the vantage point of Nagasaki at the end of the seventeenth century, Engelbert Kaempfer (see p.108) described how: 'Cherry and wild plum trees are grown only on account of their beautiful blossoms. Cultivation has produced blossoms the size of double-petalled roses and they burst forth in such quantity that they cover the whole tree like blood-drenched snow. These trees are the greatest ornament of all houses and temple gardens.'[4] The miraculous effect of the flowering cherry trees inspired folktales such as *The Tale of the Man who made Cherry Trees Bloom*, which appeared as 'The Envious Neighbour' in Andrew Lang's Violet Fairy Book of 1901, part of his great compilation of fairy tales of the world. In the story an old man possesses a special mortar that turns rice into gold. When his jealous

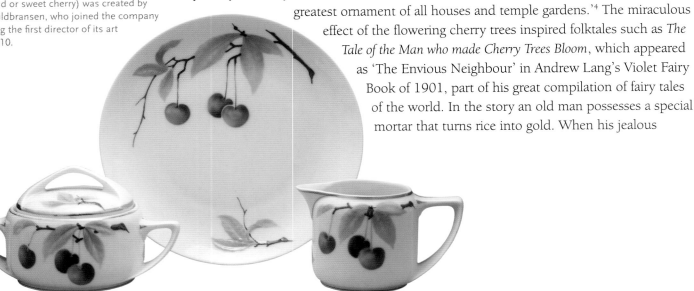

neighbour smashes and burns the mortar, the old man scatters the ashes on the bare cherry trees. This makes them blossom in the middle of winter, to the delight of a passing *daimyo* or local lord, who richly rewards the old man.

Since the late nineteenth century ornamental varieties of Japanese cherry such as *Prunus sargentii* and *Prunus speciosa*, as well as *Prunus serrulata*, have been planted in many parts of Europe and North America. Other species had long been present though; the dating of cherry stones found at archaeological sites in Europe has established consumption of *Prunus avium*, the wild or sweet cherry, from at least the third millennium BC. Together with the closely related *Prunus cerasus* (sour cherry, often known as the morello cherry), it was cultivated in south-west Asia, Turkey and Greece before it reached western Europe. According to Pliny: 'Before the victory of Lucius Lucullus in the war against Mithridates, that is down to 74 B.C., there were no cherry-trees in Italy. Lucullus first imported them from Pontus, and in 120 years they have crossed the ocean and got as far as Britain . . . Of cherries the Apronian are the reddest, and the Lutatian the blackest, while the Caecilian kind are perfectly round.'[5]

Quercus

OVER 600 species of oak, both evergreen and deciduous, grow across Europe, Asia and North, Central and South America. As a symbol of strength and endurance the tree has sustained a multitude of myths associated with local, national and imperial identity, and was sacred to gods including Zeus, king of the Greek gods, and Thor, the Norse god of thunder.

At the heart of Zeus's sanctuary at Dodona in north-western Greece – regarded as the most ancient of all the Hellenic oracles – was an ancient oak (probably a Valonia oak, *Quercus macrolepis*). According to Herodotus, legend had it that a black dove came from Thebes in Egypt and, speaking in a human voice, told the people there should be an oracle to Zeus on that spot.[1] In Homer's *Odyssey*, the hero Odysseus goes to Dodona 'to hear the will of Zeus that rustles forth from the god's tall leafy oak: how should he return, after all the years away, to his own green land of Ithaca'.[2]

Gold oak wreaths are listed in inventories from Greek temples and sanctuaries and are known from burials in Macedonia, South Italy, Asia Minor and the northern Black Sea region, including a recently excavated example of the fourth century BC from the ancient Macedonian capital of Aegae (Vergina). Oak wreaths were conferred by the Romans, a practice described by Pliny:

> In the same northern region is the vast expanse of the Hercynian oak forest, untouched by the ages and coeval with the world, which surpasses all marvels by its almost immortal destiny . . . They are practically all of the acorn-bearing class of oak, which is ever held in honour at Rome, because from it are obtained the Civic Wreaths, that glorious emblem of military valour, but now for a long time past also an emblem of the emperor's clemency . . . The Civic Wreath was first made

John Dunstall (d. 1693), A pollard oak near West Hampnett Place, Chichester. *c.* 1660. Watercolour over graphite on vellum, 13.4 x 16 cm.

Dunstall, who described himself in his will as a schoolmaster, left a manuscript for 'The Art of Delineation or Drawing. In six Books'. Trees, Flowers and Fruits were the subjects of three of the books; his emphasis was on the spiritual purpose of drawing the objects of God's creation, its benefit for the 'innocent employment it provides Ladies and Gentlewomen of Quality' and its practical use for painters, printmakers and others.

BELOW
Ship's figurehead carved in oak, found in the river Schelde in Belgium. 4th–6th century AD. H. 149 cm.

Once thought to be of Viking origin, scientific (Carbon 14) analysis has redated this to an earlier period, indicating a late Roman or Germanic context for the ship from which it came.

LEFT
Gold oak wreath with a bee and two cicadas. Hellenistic, 350–300 BC. L. 7.7 cm, diam. 23 cm.

This reputedly came from a tomb excavated in Turkey on the Dardanelles, the passage between the Aegean and the Black Sea.

John Dunstall fecit.

Palamon's Eiche.

Seinem innigst verehrten Vater, dem Goldsticker Herren Christian Wilhelm Kolbe zugeeignet.

of the leaves of the holm-oak [*Quercus ilex*, one of the evergreens], but afterwards preference was given to a wreath from chestnut-oak [probably the Valonia oak rather than *Quercus casteinfolia* [castaneifolia] or chestnut-leaved oak], which is sacred to Jove.[3]

Acorns were important for economic as well as symbolic reasons, particularly, according to Pliny, in the Spanish provinces, where they were dried and ground into flour for bread and served at table: 'Acorns at this very day constitute the wealth of many races, even when they are enjoying peace.'[4]

The 'Hercynian oak forest', to which Pliny referred, extended across what is now southern Germany, from the Black Forest in the west to the Carpathian Mountains in the east. This was but a portion of the ancient forests that became so important a part of German cultural and national identity in the eighteenth and nineteenth centuries. A key figure in the creation of this identity was the heroic Hermann, a Germanic chieftain who defeated the Romans in the forest in AD 9. The historian Tacitus's account (*c*. AD 120)

Carl Wilhelm Kolbe (1759–1835), *Palamon's Oak*. 1798. Etching, 57.8 x 74.2 cm.

The subject was taken from an idyll of the same name by the highly regarded Swiss writer and poet Salomon Gessner (1730–88). Idas and Mycon, two goatherds resting in the shade of the tree, recall the virtue of Palamon who long ago had prayed to the god Pan that his scanty flock might be increased so that he could both sacrifice to Pan and have enough sheep to share with his neighbour. When his prayer was answered Palamon planted the oak consecrating it to Pan.

was the basis of three odes by the poet F.G. Klopstock (1724–1803), the best known being *Hermannsschlacht* (Hermann's Battle) of 1767. When Prussia with Austria and Russia defeated Napoleon at the Battle of Leipzig in 1813, the parallel with Hermann's victory was immediately invoked; during the War of Liberation and afterwards the forest became a symbol of freedom and unity.

The German printmaker C.W. Kolbe had an intense relationship with trees, earning him the nickname *Eichenkolbe* ('Oak Kolbe'). He wrote, 'It is trees that have made me an artist – if there were no trees in paradise I wouldn't give a penny for my peace of mind'.[5] Again, his visual preoccupations with the forest went hand in hand with an all-encompassing sense of German identity. In 1806–9, during the Napoleonic Wars, Kolbe published an essay comparing the German and French languages. His intention was to prove that German had a naturally expressive power that made it one of the *Ursprache*, or original languages of mankind, superior to the artificial refinements of a romance language such as French. From Kolbe's pastoral vision of densely foliated sylvan glades to the solitary, often bare trees of Caspar David Friedrich's landscapes, the oak became a key element in the pictorial vocabulary of German Romanticism.

In Britain the 'oak groves of Albion', as evoked in William Blake's poem *Jerusalem*, were mainly populated with *Quercus robur* (pedunculate oak) and *Quercus petraea* (sessile or durmast oak). At the end of the seventeenth century new species, *Quercus prinus* (chestnut oak) and *Quercus coccinea* (scarlet oak), were introduced from north-eastern America, but they did not carry the symbolism associated with what were regarded as their 'native' counterparts. Robert Herrick's poem 'To Anthea' (1633) refers to the ancient custom of 'beating the bounds' (boundaries) of a parish; if an oak tree was incorporated into the bounds then a gospel had to be read at the tree (hence the place-name 'Gospel Oak'):

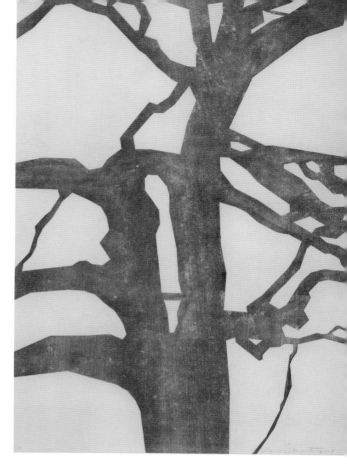

ABOVE
David Rabinowitch (b. 1943), *Altan: Ruthe*, from a set of three prints. 2004. Woodcut, 69 x 50 cm.

The artist is a Canadian sculptor, printmaker and draughtsman who has worked in Europe, mainly in Germany, since 1972. The three *Altan* portfolios from 2002–4, with a total of thirteen woodcuts, were inspired by ancient oaks that grow near the artist's home in Wiesbaden. On Mount Nero, overlooking Wiesbaden, are stands of oak said to be 1000 years old, while in the north of the province of Hesse at Rheinhardswald is one of the largest forest regions in Germany, renowned for its oaks and beeches.

LEFT
Oak leaf tiara, with diamonds set into silver and gold. *c.* 1855. W. 4.8 cm (central spray); W. 9.3 cm (outer sprays and comb mounts); 16.3 cm (circlet).

The wreath comes apart into three sprays which can be reconfigured on different frames to make one large corsage brooch or two combs for the hair. The initials and coronet on the box suggest that the set may have belonged to Mary Viscountess Portman, quite possibly a gift made on the occasion of her wedding in 1855 when she was nineteen. Young girls did not wear diamonds until they were married and oak meant fidelity because of its strength.[6]

Dearest, bury me,
Under that holy oak, or gospel-tree,
Where, (though thou see'st not), thou mayst,
Think upon
Me, when you yearly go'st Procession.

Notwithstanding the oak's cherished status, like other trees it has been the victim of its manifold usefulness, from the Bronze Age, when whole trunks were hollowed out to make log boats for navigating inland waterways, and the Romans' depletion of the oak forests of southern England to provide timber for shipbuilding and charcoal for metal extraction. The situation that Evelyn deplored in *Sylva* in 1664 (see pp. 19–20) was a national emergency. The replenishment of oak stocks was a constant theme and subject of debate, for example in James Wheeler's book *The Modern Druid containing Instructions for the much better culture of Young Oaks* (1747). The navy was literally the oak's downfall, but together they made a powerful national symbol. The song *Heart of Oak*, written by the actor David Garrick with music composed by William Boyce, first performed in 1759, became the official march of the Royal Navy.

In 1664 Charles II made a visit 'to Blackwall and viewed the dock and the new Wet dock, which is newly made there, and a brave new merchantman which is to be launched shortly, and they say to be called the Royal Oak', as recorded by Samuel Pepys. HMS *Royal Oak*, launched at Portsmouth the same year, was named in honour of the oak tree at Boscobel in which Charles II hid after his defeat at the Battle of Worcester in 1651. It spawned a host of inns of the same name, and after the Restoration Charles's birthday, 29 May, was celebrated as 'Oak Apple Day'. The oak was associated with the 'legitimate' constitution of Britain overthrown by Cromwell. In a satirical print of 1649 directed against the execution of Charles I, Cromwell was depicted standing at the mouth of hell, ordering the destruction of 'The Royall Oake of Brittayne'. An oak tree with its top cut off was a sign of mourning for Charles I, while a young sapling springing from the roots of a stricken oak tree, with the word 'REVIRESCIT' (It flourishes anew), became the emblem of the

THE ROYALL OAKE OF BRITTAYNE

Jacobite cause in the eighteenth century. A sentimental allegiance to the oak continued even after the defeat of the 'Young Pretender' Bonnie Prince Charlie at Culloden in 1746. The 'Revirescit' image appears on Jacobite commemorative drinking glasses, and on a medal commissioned by the members of the Oak Society, which met at the Crown and Anchor by St Clement Dane's Church on the Strand in London. The medal was doubtless intended to raise funds for Prince Charles James Edward, who secretly visited London in 1750, staying near the Strand. He conferred with Jacobites, including a faction within the Church of England with whom he took Communion to show his willingness to serve as a Protestant monarch, and even considered an assault on the Tower of London, but deemed there was insufficient support.

The Druids were identified by Pliny as 'what they [in the Gallic provinces] call their magicians . . . they hold nothing more sacred than mistletoe and a tree on which it is growing, provided it is a Valonia oak'.[7] Interest in the history of the indigenous inhabitants of the British Isles was stoked in the seventeenth and eighteenth centuries by the power of ancient monuments such as Stonehenge, and the romantic appeal of the 'Celtic fringe', those regions that retain elements of their Celtic heritage. By the late eighteenth century there was a sizeable body of literature hailing the supposed philosophical, poetic and scientific achievements of the Druids and their veneration for nature's mysteries.[8] Freemasonry inspired the creation of Druidic societies which shared the former's ideals and love of ritual. The magic flute of Mozart's opera (first performed in 1791), with its many layered references to the symbolism of Freemasonry, is said by Pamina to be made from a 1000-year-old oak, as she hands it to Tamino. The Ancient Order of Druids was founded in London in 1781; in 1833 its membership split between the majority, who wanted to retain its purpose as a friendly society, to provide benefits for members and their families, and those of more mystical leanings. The first group

ABOVE
Thomas Toft (d. 1689), Slipware dish showing Charles II hiding in an oak tree, flanked by the lion and the unicorn, the heraldic creatures denoting the English crown. 1670–80. Diam. 50.5 cm.

Toft, whose work has become greatly admired, is thought to have worked in Staffordshire around 1671–89. He died a pauper and was buried in Stoke on Trent.

160

Edmund Marriner Gill (1820–94), Oak tree near Finchley. 1853. Watercolour, 24.8 x 15.3 cm.

Gill began as a portraitist but changed to landscape after meeting the painter David Cox in Birmingham in 1841. He exhibited at the Royal Academy from 1842 to 1886, earning the nickname 'Waterfall Gill'. Finchley in Middlesex was then a village on one of the main routes into London from the north. One of the 'landmark' oak trees there was named Turpin's Oak after the highwayman executed in York in 1739.

withdrew to form the United Ancient Order of Druids (still extant), which by 1846 had 330 lodges in England and Wales and several overseas.

Oak, ash (p. 104) and thorn (p. 174) were seen as a magical trio in the flourishing Celtic folklore of the nineteenth century and beyond, rooting the identity of the British Isles in a period that preceded foreign invasions by the Romans and then the Normans. This romantic view informs Rudyard Kipling's *Tree Poem* at the beginning of his historical fiction for children, *Puck of Pook's Hill* (1906):

> Of all the trees that grow so fair
> Old England to adorn
> Greater are none beneath the Sun,
> Than Oak and Ash and Thorn
>
> Oak of the Clay lived many a day,
> Or ever Aeneas began;
> Ash of the Loam was a lady at home,
> When Brut was an outlaw man;
> Thorn of the Down saw New Troy Town
> (From which was London born);
> Witness hereby the ancientry
> Of Oak and Ash and Thorn!

David Garrick, the writer of *Heart of Oak*, was a prime mover in establishing Shakespeare's position as the 'national poet' of England. Among the many relics associated with this 'cult' in the nineteenth century were those made from the timber of an oak tree in Home Park, Windsor, which was linked to the ghost of Herne the Hunter in *The Merry Wives of Windsor* (Act IV, Scene IV). In 1791 William Gilpin (see p. 54) 'identified' the tree, which was toppled in a gale in 1863. Its importance was such that Queen Victoria presented a piece of the wood to the British Museum and had a cabinet made from the tree. William Perry, a wood carver, was given some fragments of the tree on a visit to Windsor, from which he made various memorabilia, including a casket to hold a first folio of Shakespeare in 1866 (now in the Folger Shakespeare Library, Washington DC). The following year he published *A treatise on the Identity of Herne's Oak shewing the Maiden Tree to have been the real one*, his vindication of the 'authenticity' of the tree.

ABOVE
Rev. Matthew William Peters (1741/2–1814), Scene from *The Merry Wives of Windsor* with Falstaff as Herne the Hunter. *c.* 1793. Watercolour, 34.7 x 44.5 cm.

The composition is probably a study for one of the prints from Macklin's Shakespeare Gallery on 1793.

BELOW
Block of oak from Herne's Oak in Windsor Great Park, mentioned in Shakespeare's *The Merry Wives of Windsor*. 51.5 x 45 cm.

Salix

By the rivers of Babylon, there we
sat down, yea we wept, when we
remembered Zion.
We hanged our harps upon the willows in the midst thereof.
Psalm 137 verses 1–2, Authorised version

The Political Weeping Willow, 13 May 1791.
Hand-coloured etching published by William
Holland (1757–1815). 31.3 x 24.7 cm.

This image satirizes a famous event that
took place in the House of Commons on
6 May 1791, when Charles James Fox wept
copiously at Edmund Burke's renunciation
of their friendship because of Fox's praise
for the French Revolution. Burke repudiated
him, declaring 'there is something in the
cursed French Constitution which envenoms
everything'.

THE POLITICAL WEEPING WILLOW.

162

SALIX BABYLONICA, commonly known as the weeping willow, has become a universal
symbol of grief and loss. The name '*babylonica*' derived from its mention in the biblical
account of the Jewish exile in Babylon, quoted above. Along with many other species of
willow, it is indigenous to western China and was only introduced to Europe in the late
seventeenth century. First recorded in England in 1748 (being grown by a
Mr Vernon at Twickenham), it has largely disappeared in the United Kingdom because
of its susceptibility to frost. The weeping willow most widely grown today is a cultivar,
'Chrysocoma', of *Salix x. sepulcralis*, itself a hybrid of the Chinese *Salix babylonica* and
the European *Salix alba* (white willow).

Willows belong to the same family (Salicaceae) as sallows, osiers
and poplars (see p. 142), trees that are fast-growing and easy to
propagate in a wide range of soils and climatic conditions. *Salix alba* and
Salix fragilis (crack willow) are most commonly found in northern
Europe. Their timber is used to make baskets and cricket bats, and they
are often planted along riverbanks and canals to prevent erosion. When
Leonardo da Vinci was looking at ways to convert the river Adda in
Lombardy (which formed the border between the Duchy of Milan and
the Republic of Venice) into a canal, he observed that, far from damaging
riverbanks, willow roots actually reinforced them. For the same reason
willows are a commonplace of the Dutch landscape, as captured by
Rembrandt and Van Gogh. Pollarding is a method of pruning to inhibit
the tree's size. Rembrandt's St Jerome is seated beside a pollard willow,
therefore the setting is that of a 'managed' landscape, rather than the
desert or wilderness chosen by other artists for their representations of
the penitent fourth-century saint (for example, Dürer's print of 1512).

Native Americans used willow (for example *Salix exigua*, narrowleaf,
sandbar or coyote willow), both to make things and for medicinal purposes;
its inner bark is a source of salicin, the active ingredient in aspirin (first
patented in 1897), which eases pain and reduces inflammation. The
strength, pliability and lightness of willow twigs make them ideal for

Rembrandt van Rijn (1606–69), *St Jerome beside a pollard willow*. 1648. Etching and drypoint, 18 x 13.3 cm.

163

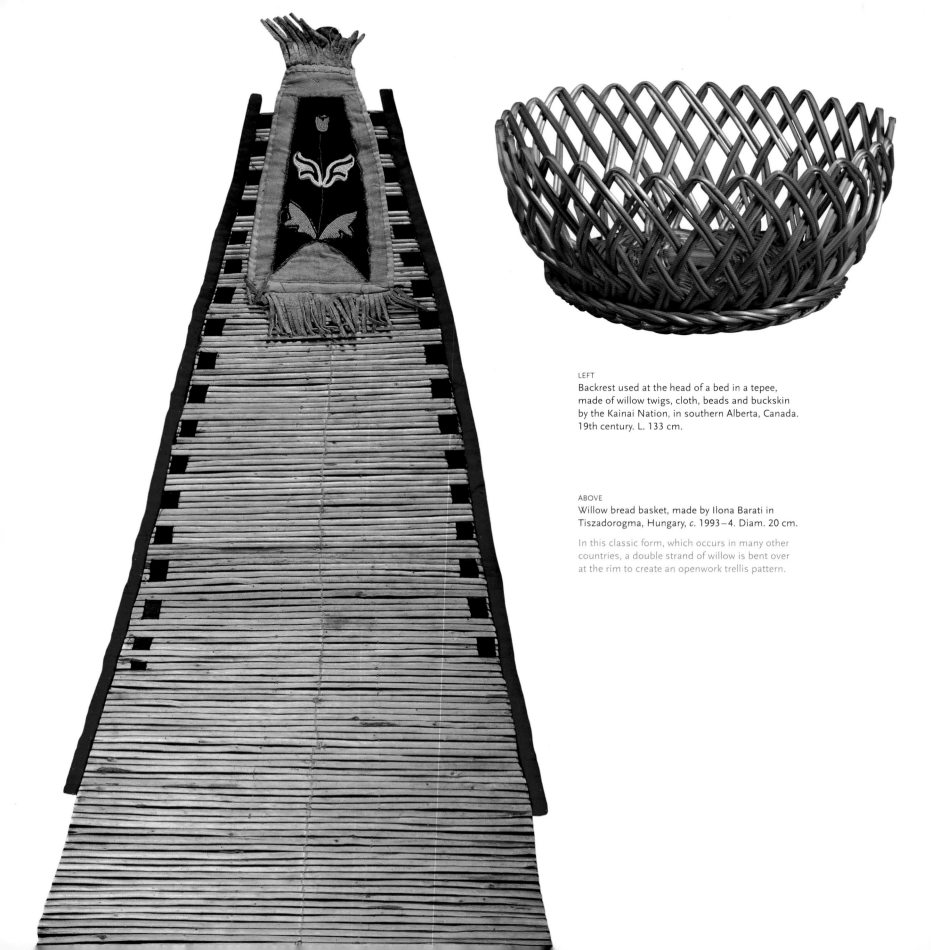

LEFT
Backrest used at the head of a bed in a tepee,
made of willow twigs, cloth, beads and buckskin
by the Kainai Nation, in southern Alberta, Canada.
19th century. L. 133 cm.

ABOVE
Willow bread basket, made by Ilona Barati in
Tiszadorogma, Hungary, c. 1993–4. Diam. 20 cm.

In this classic form, which occurs in many other
countries, a double strand of willow is bent over
at the rim to create an openwork trellis pattern.

basketry, cradleboards and backrests. The leaves of *Salix discolor* (American willow or American pussy willow), one of the species native to Canada and the north-eastern United States from Maine to Maryland, were employed by engravers as part of an anti-counterfeiting device for paper currency. From 1730 Benjamin Franklin printed notes issued by the states of Pennsylvania, New Jersey and Delaware. In 1739 he started reproducing images of leaves on the reverse of the note, influenced by the naturalist and engraver Joseph Breintnall, who made 'nature prints' directly from inked leaves that were run through the press inside folded sheets of paper. Franklin's argument was that no counterfeiter would be able to imitate exactly the patterns of the originals which, as Breintnall had claimed for his own 'nature prints', were 'Engraven by the Greatest and best Engraver in the Universe'.

In China the willow is regarded as the symbol of light and enemy of darkness, and its branches are hung over doorways at Chinese New Year to ward off evil spirits. It is an attribute of Guanyin, the Goddess of Mercy, who is often shown with a willow branch in a vase of water at her side (see p. 34). Though inspired by a taste for 'Chinoiserie', willow pattern china has no other connection with Chinese culture or ceramics, but was the name given to a transfer pattern that was printed in a number of colours on white earthenware. The English potter Thomas Minton is credited with its introduction in 1790. His factory and other imitators made it into one of the most popular lines ever produced, inventing narratives around the features of the 'Chinese' garden to promote sales of the china.

Thirty-five Dollars

Printed by H A L L and
SELLERS. 1779.

Taxus

There is a Yew-tree, pride of Lorton Vale,
Which to this day stands single, in the midst
Of its own darkness, as it stood of yore:
Not loathe to furnish weapons for the Bands
Of Umfraville or Percy ere they marched
To Scotland's heaths; or those that crossed the sea
And drew their sounding bows at Azincour, [. . .]
Of vast circumference and gloom profound
This solitary Tree! -a living thing
Produced too slowly ever to decay;
   William Wordsworth, *Yew-Trees* (1803, published 1815)

IN THIS POEM Wordsworth goes on to extol 'those Fraternal Four of Borrowdale / Joined in one solemn and capacious grove'. The antiquity, solemnity and often melancholic associations of the common yew (*Taxus baccata*) have made it one of the most memorable trees in northern Europe. It is often seen in churchyards in Britain and France, though the trees are frequently much older than the churches themselves. The yew's association with death stems from Greek mythology, as it was one of the trees in Persephone's grove at the mouth of the underworld, Hades. However, despite its tendency to kill all that tries to grow within its shade, the yew's symbolism in Britain is also that of resurrection because of its evergreen foliage, rather than of death alone.

At between 2000 and 5000 years old, the oldest tree in the United Kingdom is the Fortingall Yew by Loch Tay in Scotland. It was first measured in 1769 by the antiquary and naturalist Daines Barrington, and was found to have a girth of fifty-two feet. Another ancient yew which has captured popular imagination in Britain is the Harlington Yew, estimated at 900 years old; its proximity to Heathrow airport has been used by conservationists as one of the arguments against a third runway. In the eighteenth century it was depicted in 'topiarized' form, accompanied by a poem by John Saxy, the 'shaver' responsible for the tree's fantastical shapes:

Masters, if you approve these Lays
And shaver Saxy design to praise,
Crown him with Yew instead of Bays [see bay laurel, p. 112]
Be kind to John your Tree who Trims
With easy Rhimes but aching Limbs.

Taxus baccata
Yew Tree

Trade card of Thomas Waring, bow and arrow maker. 1806. Engraving, 11.6 x 7.5 cm.

Thomas Waring's premises were off Bedford Square, close to the British Museum. The card is from the collection formed by Sarah Sophia Banks (1744–1818), the sister of Sir Joseph Banks (see p. 10).

(see p. 10)

168

FAR RIGHT
Wooden percussion instrument for striking wooden boards, made by Nuu-chah-nulth (Northwest Coast peoples) from Nootka Sound, British Columbia. 1780 or before. L. 32 cm.

The main body of the instrument is a single branch and trunk section of yew (*Taxus brevifolia*), together with spruce root (probably *Picea sitchensis*, Sitka spruce) and cedar bark (probably *Thuja plicata*, western or Pacific red cedar). Captain Cook made landfall beside the stretch of water that he called King George's Sound in 1778 on his third and final Pacific voyage; it was renamed Nootka Sound in the 1780s. The instrument, believed to be one of only two surviving examples, was presented to the British Museum by Sir Joseph Banks.

RIGHT
Painted club, carved in yew wood in the form of an animal, made by Tlingit people in Alaska. 19th century. L. 56 cm.

The first Europeans to have contact with the Tlingit were Russians, in 1741. Alaska came under United States jurisdiction in 1867 with the Treaty of Cession.

Topiary was very fashionable in Britain in the seventeenth century, but became the butt of satire when Alexander Pope published an essay on 'Verdant Sculpture' in *The Guardian* in September 1713. Among the mock catalogue of the works in question he mentions 'Adam and Eve in yew; Adam a little shattered by the fall of the tree of knowledge in the great storm; Eve and the serpent very flourishing.' He continues, 'We seem to make it our study to recede from nature, not only in various tonsure of greens into the most regular and formal shapes but even in monstrous attempts beyond the reach of the art itself'. Pope, if not John Saxy, would be relieved to see the Harlington Yew in its 'untonsured' state today.

The tensile strength of the yew's wood made it ideal for the manufacture of longbows. However, high demand depleted stocks to such an extent that, by the end of the thirteenth century, bow staves were being imported to England. Similar shortages occurred across northern Europe, where the stocks were never adequately replenished, even after the longbow was supplanted in battle by firearms. The revival of archery as a sporting pastime in the late eighteenth century, for women as well as men, created a new demand that again was satisfied through imported yew from Spain and Italy.

The Pacific yew (*Taxus brevifolia*) grows along the coast of the north-western United States and Canada. Its wood has been used by Native Americans for all manner of items, from bows, gunstocks and canoe paddles to furniture and musical instruments. Its resistance to decay is one of its great attributes, another is its medicinal use. Modern pharmacology has benefited from the properties of *Taxus brevifolia*'s needles and bark, which are a source of taxol, a component of anti-cancer drugs.

Helen Allingham (1848–1926), Yew Tree, Northfield, near Birmingham. Brush drawing in grey ink, 19 x 13.7 cm.

Helen Allingham moved to Birmingham after the death of her father in 1862. She studied at the Birmingham School of Design before entering the Royal Academy Schools in London, one of the first women to do so. She made a considerable reputation as an illustrator and painter of rural scenes in watercolour.

169

Theobroma cacao

WHAT FIRST made its appearance as the tribute and tipple of an emperor became the perquisite of the fashionable and well-to-do in early modern Europe, playing a significant role in the fortunes of the man who founded the British Museum, Hans Sloane. Native to tropical America, the cacao tree was cultivated by the Mayas and the Mexica (Aztecs), for whom chocolate was a royal beverage believed to be of divine origin ('*Theobroma*', the first part of the tree's Linnaean name, derives from the Greek for 'food of the gods'). After toasting and milling the cacao beans, the drink was prepared by adding water to them and beating the mixture rapidly with gold, silver or wooden spoons, before pouring it from a height to produce a foamy solution. Served cold and sometimes mixed with milled corn, aromatic spices or honey, the chocolate was presented in fine gold cups to Moctezuma, the supreme ruler of Tenochtitlan (Mexico City) from 1502 to 1520. Cacao beans were used as currency and as tribute in Moctezuma's empire, and by the Spanish conquerors. The Kingsborough Codex, a Mexican pictorial manuscript in the British Museum which records the tributes paid to the Spaniards up to 1550, mentions among the many goods demanded by Gonzalo de Salazar, a Spanish governor of Mexico City, when returning to Spain in 1526: '16,000 grains of cacao, ground ready for drinking, 400 pairs of shoes, 200 jars and 40 painted chocolate cups.'

Cocoa (the name of the drink, not the plant) was thus introduced to Europe in the sixteenth century and became a popular beverage for the well-to-do (high import duties restricted its consumption), often taken as a physic to settle the stomach. Drinking chocolate grew in popularity in England from the mid-seventeenth century. The earliest establishment to serve the drink opened in Oxford in 1650, followed in 1657 by the first in London, at Bishopsgate. Two chocolate houses in the

Maria Sibylla Merian (1647–1717), Cacao pods and leaves, from an album of 91 drawings entitled *Merian's Drawings of Surinam Insects &c*, which belonged to Sir Hans Sloane. 1701–5. Watercolour with pen and ink and grey chalk on vellum, 36 x 28.2 cm

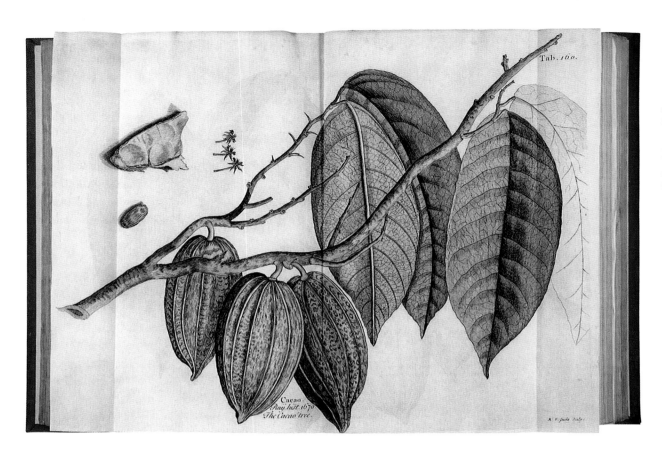

Michael van der Gucht (1660–1725), Cacao pods and leaves, after a drawing by Edward Kickius, for Sir Hans Sloane's *Natural History of Jamaica*, vol. II, 1725, pl. 160 (House of Commons Library, on loan to the British Museum).

London area of St James, White's (founded 1693) and the Cocoa Tree (founded 1698), were favoured meeting-places in the eighteenth century for supporters of the Tory party, an association that White's maintains to this day. After a while they became members' clubs, more concerned with gambling than with drinking chocolate.

Hans Sloane's first-hand acquaintance with the cacao tree and its products came when he travelled in Jamaica in 1687 as the personal physician of the Governor, the 2nd Duke of Albemarle. He described it in the second volume of *The Natural History of Jamaica* (1725): 'The harvest of the Nut is usually in *January*, or *May*; they cut the kernels out, cleanse them from their Slime, and cure them, drying them in the Sun on Sheets or Mats . . . To make Drink the Indians dry them [the kernels] on an earthen Tile, grind them with Stones to Powder, and mix it with Water and Pepper, which makes a Dish fitter for Swine than Men.' In the interests of making a dish fit for men, as opposed to 'swine', Sloane devised a successful recipe for milk chocolate, later acquired by the firm of Cadbury. He was not the first to think of adding milk; that was mentioned in the 1662 book *Indian nectar; or a discourse concerning chocolate*, published by Henry Stubbe, who later became the King's Physician for Jamaica.

John Chartier (fl. 1698–1731), The Palmerston gold chocolate cups. Made in London *c.* 1700 for Anne Houblon, later Viscountess Palmerston. who died in 1735. H. 6.5 cm.

Chocolate cups were themselves luxury items, most particularly this pair, bequeathed by Viscountess Palmerston to her husband Henry Temple, 1st Viscount Palmerston (*c.* 1673–1757), and described in her will of 4 September 1726 as 'the 2 lesser Chocolate Cups you would sometimes look on as a Remembrance of Death, and also of the fondest and Faithfullest Friend you ever had'. The family tradition was that they were made from melted-down mourning rings. The bases and inside of the handles are inscribed 'Sacred to the departed' and 'He has not deserved sweet who has not tasted bitter' on one, and 'Let us drink to the dead' and 'Think on yr friends and Death as the chief' on the other.

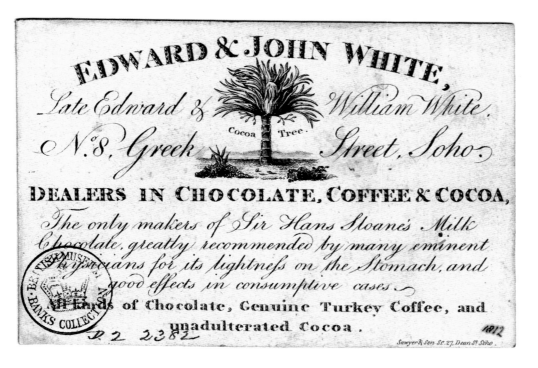

Richard Sawyer (fl. 1807–19), Trade card of Edward & John White, 'No. 8, Greek Street, Soho. Dealers in Chocolate, Coffee & Cocoa. The only makers of Sir Hans Sloane's Milk Chocolate, greatly recommended by many eminent Physicians for its lightness on the Stomach, and good effects in consumptive cases. All kinds of Chocolate, Genuine Turkey Coffee, And unadulterated Cocoa.' c. 1812. Engraving, 6.1 x 9 cm.

Daniel Oblie (b. 1960), Wooden model coffin in the form of a cacao pod, made at 'Hello Furniture Works' in Teshie, Ghana. L. 35 cm.

Model coffins are made by employees of the coffin workshops and sold by them to make extra money. Coffins in the form of cacao pods are often made for cacao planters. Africa's most successful cacao co-operative, Kupa Kokoo (Good Farmers' Company), was set up in Ghana in 1993, and has become the main source of Fairtrade chocolate.

 172

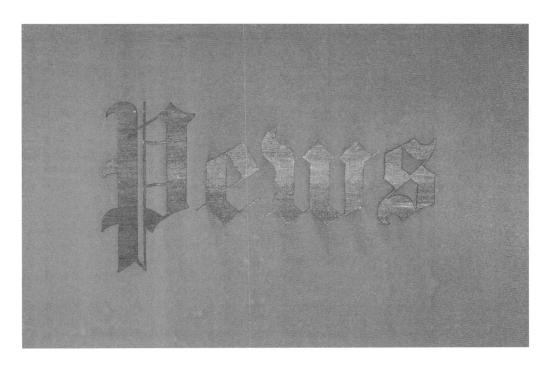

LEFT
Ed Ruscha (b. 1937), *Pews*, from *News, Mews, Pews, Brews, Stews and Dues*, a portfolio of seven screenprints printed in organic inks and published by Editions Alecto in 1970. *Pews* was printed in Hershey's chocolate flavour syrup, Camp coffee and chicory essence, 45.6 x 68.6 cm.

One of America's leading Pop artists, Ruscha created a room filled with sheets screenprinted in chocolate paste for the United States pavilion at the Venice Biennale in 1970.

BELOW
Pottery figure of a chocolate sauce seller. Pueblas, Mexico, 1980s. H. 4.5 cm.

Even more remarkable than Sloane in terms of documenting exotic plants was Maria Sibylla Merian, an artist and naturalist from Frankfurt who made an expedition between 1699 and 1701 to the Dutch colony of Surinam in South America. Her interest lay primarily with the insects but, in illustrating them on what she considered to be their food plants, she also provided an exquisite botanical record. Of the cacao tree she noted: 'These trees grow very well in Surinam, although they are difficult to cultivate because they must always be protected underneath another tree to shelter them from the sun.'

Theobroma cacao is of great importance to the livelihood of small farmers in many of the world's poorest countries in Africa and the Americas. Current scientific research is further revealing the plant's potential. In 2010 researchers completed the DNA sequence of a variety of *Theobroma cacao* called *Criollo*, first domesticated by the Maya around 3,000 years ago, and used to make fine dark chocolate. Among the 28,798 genes identified are those that help to guard against disease, as well as ones that make cocoa butter, a key ingredient in cosmetics and drugs.

Ziziphus

Ziziphus mauritania (Jujube, Chinese apple, Indian plum). Company School painting from an album of 58 botanical subjects. Early 19th century. Bodycolour, 49.2 x 32.9 cm.

The paintings in this album are linked to some commissioned from native artists by William Roxburgh during his time as Superintendant of the Calcutta Botanic Garden from 1793 to 1813. Founded in 1787 by Colonel Kyd of the East India Company, the Botanic Garden had the support of Sir Joseph Banks at Kew, who saw its potential for 'the promotion of public utility and science'. Roxburgh greatly expanded the range of plants; the record he instigated was the basis of the first comprehensive survey of the flora of India, *Flora Indica*, published after his death in 1820 and 1824.

THE SMALL spiny trees of the various species of *Ziziphus* produce one of the world's major fruit crops, the jujube fruit. Cultivated for several thousand years across many parts of Asia and the eastern Mediterranean, they are of value for their strong wood, medicinal properties, as a source of honey and for being a host to the lac insect, which makes a resin used for polish and lacquer. According to Pliny: 'The region of the Cyrenaica [eastern coastal region of Libya] ranks the lotus [*Ziziphus lotus*] below its own Christ's-thorn [*Ziziphus spina-christi*]. This is more in the nature of a shrub, and its fruit is redder, and contains a kernel that is eaten by itself, as it is agreeable alone; it is improved by being dipped in wine, and moreover its juice improves wine'.[1]

The species *Ziziphus spina-christi*, mentioned in the Qur'an (see p. 35), is revered by Muslims as the *sidr* tree. For this reason it is often an important feature of Islamic gardens; it was used in 2010 as the inaugural plant in a garden at Doha, Qatar. It grows in abundance around Jerusalem, and was believed to have been used to make the Crown of Thorns, which – with the Cross – became the most eloquent symbol of Christ's suffering and sacrifice. The association has lost none of its resonance in modern times. Responding to the Second World War and its aftermath, the artist Graham Sutherland evoked the Crown of Thorns in his series of 'thorn head' paintings. These were inspired by a commission in 1946 to paint the Crucifixion for St Matthew's church in Northampton, and by photographs of concentration camp victims. In Sutherland's landscape compositions, thorn trees became what he called 'a sort of paraphrase of the *Crucifixion* and the *Crucified Head* – the cruelty'.

The Crown of Thorns was first mentioned as a relic in Jerusalem in the early fifth century, and further references were made to its presence there over the next five hundred years. It was later transferred to Constantinople, capital of the Eastern Roman empire, where it formed part of the greatest concentration of Christian relics ever assembled. After the sack of that city during the Fourth Crusade in 1204, many of these relics were pawned or sold. Between 1239 and 1241 the King of France, Louis XI (St Louis), acquired the Crown of Thorns, portions of the True Cross and other relics of Christ's Passion, and brought them back to Paris where the Sainte Chapelle was built to house them. Although the chapel was looted during the French Revolution, the Crown, a portion of the True Cross, and one of the nails believed to have secured Christ to the Cross, survived. These relics were moved in 1801 to the Cathedral of Notre-Dame as part of Napoleon's Concordat with the Papacy. They continue to be displayed there on the first Friday of each month, every Friday in Lent and on Good Friday.

Odilon Redon (1840–1916),
Head of Christ wearing the
Crown of Thorns. 1894–5.
Charcoal, black pastel and
black crayon, 52.2 x 37.9 cm.

Redon made a number of
drawings of this subject,
which fitted with his interest
in visionary heads and ideas
of transcendence; however,
he resisted the labelling
of his compositions as
Christian art. This drawing
was bought from Redon in
1895 by an English patron,
Dr Albert Edward Tebb, with
whom the artist stayed in
London in the same year.

The Holy Thorn Reliquary, made
c. 1390–1400. Gold, enamel and
precious stones, H. 30.5 cm.

The reliquary, commissioned by Jean,
duc de Berry (1340–1416), to hold a
single thorn, presents a sumptuous
vision of the Last Judgement, with
God the Father and Christ in Majesty
looking down on angelic trumpeters.
The duke built a Sainte Chapelle
attached to his palace at Bourges to
house this and other relics, along
with his tomb.

The Crown received by Notre-Dame was a circlet of twisted Baltic rushes (*Juncus balticus*), into which thorns from *Ziziphus spina-christi* had once been woven, making it easy to detach individual specimens for presentation as gifts of the highest distinction. Such thorns were in circulation long before the Crown was acquired by Louis XI. While the relic was still in Jerusalem, the Byzantine empress Irene made a gift of thorns to Charlemagne, King of the Franks. He deposited them at Aachen, where he was crowned Holy Roman Emperor in AD 800. Louis XI presented many more of these gifts, especially to members of the French royal family, and they continued to be passed along the genealogical line. The sumptuous Holy Thorn Reliquary, illustrated here, was made at the end of the fourteenth century to house a thorn given to Jean, duc de Berry, by his brother Charles V of France.[2] Another reliquary in the British Museum, in the form of a pendant, also contains a holy thorn. It dates from *c.* 1340 and is associated with Philip VI of France and his queen, Jeanne de Bourgogne. A third holy thorn at the Jesuit college of Stonyhurst, in the north of England, was owned by Mary Queen of Scots, who was given a double thorn in 1558 on her marriage to the French dauphin (later François II, d. 1560). The thorn was divided when presented to the Society of Jesus in 1594 and two separate reliquaries were made. The one at Stonyhurst contains what was supposed to be a string of Mary's pearls, thereby making it into a devotional object that linked the execution of Mary to the suffering of Christ.

The celebration of the Festival of the Holy Thorn, together with votive masses to the Crown of Thorns, was a feature of English religious life in the early Tudor period. Around 1526–30 the composer John Taverner (*c.* 1490–1545) wrote a mass titled *Missa Corona spinea*, though he became an ardent reformer only a few years later, following Henry VIII's repudiation of papal authority in 1536. The symbolic power of the Crown of Thorns was most famously invoked in post-Reformation Britain by the frontispiece to the book purported to be Charles I's last testament, *Eikon Basilike* (The Royal Portrait), published on 9 February 1649, ten days after his execution. The image of Charles taking hold of a crown of thorns, gazing towards a heavenly crown of glory while his earthly crown lies rejected at his feet, was a piece of consummate propaganda. The publication ran to thirty-six editions in 1649 alone, prompting Parliament to commission a counter-attack from John Milton, *Eikonklastes* (The Icon Breaker).

Jacobus van Huysum (1687/9–1740), *Christ's Thorn*. Watercolour over graphite, 37.5 x 26.5 cm.

From an album of drawings of plants whose names were registered at monthly meetings of a Society of Gardeners in London from *c.* 1723 onwards (see p. 16).

LEFT
William Marshall (fl. 1617–49), frontispiece to *Eikon Basilike*. 1649. Etching and engraving, 26.6 x 16.7 cm.

177

EPILOGUE *Where have all the forests gone?*

They took all the trees
Put 'em in a tree museum
And they charged the people
A dollar and a half just to see 'em

Don't it always seem to go
That you don't know what you've got
Till it's gone
They paved paradise
And put up a parking lot.
    Joni Mitchell, *Big Yellow Taxi* (1970)[1]

NOTWITHSTANDING mankind's desire to romanticize the forest, to animate it with spirits and to revere its trees collectively and individually, human history has been one of constant deforestation and all too little by way of compensation. Whether paving paradise for a parking lot, felling trees for fuel, ship's timbers and other building purposes, for railway construction or for paper, clearing land for agriculture, cattle grazing or extractive industries, almost no place or period has been spared such depredation. The metal industry in Bronze Age Cyprus collapsed because of the eventual lack of suitable fuel; Plato's *Critias* (*c.* 360 BC) described the deforestation of the hills around Athens to satisfy the navy's demand for wood, and how the treeless land could no longer retain the rainfall, the water running off the bare earth into the sea. Artemis was the Greek goddess of the forests, yet the environment around her shrine at Ephesus was degraded, and the Romans deforested many areas, large parts of North Africa and southern England to name but two.

Ronald Pennell (b. 1935), *A Tree for Me*: bronze medal.
1985. Diam. 4.9 cm.

The artist has written that the obverse of the medal shows 'a man wheeling away the last ancient tree in a wheelbarrow perhaps for preservation in a museum! The serpent, with all it represents in mythology and Christianity, observes all. On the reverse three dead trees in a barren landscape. I am an optimist, but everyone alive today must think from time to time – where, when and how will it end?' (quoted in Mark Jones, *Contemporary British Medals*, London 1986, p. 51).

Sandstone architectural
bracket carved in the shape
of a *yakṣī* clasping a tree.
1st century AD. H. 65 cm.

A *yakṣī* was a minor
deity associated with
auspiciousness. The bracket
comes from the Great Stupa
at Sanchi, the Buddhist
reliquary mound north
of Bhopal in the state of
Madhya Pradesh in India.
She is embracing the Sal or
Shala tree (*Shorea robusta*)
which will cause it to burst
into bloom, a reference to
a pre-Buddhist fertility rite
which helped to ensure the
auspiciousness of the site.

Aesop's fable *The Trees and the Axe* is the cautionary tale of a woodman who went into a forest and begged the trees for a handle for his axe. The principal trees at once agreed to the request and unhesitatingly gave him a young ash sapling. No sooner had he made the required handle than he set to work to fell the very same trees that had made this sacrifice of another. When they saw the use to which he was putting their gift, they cried, "Alas! alas! We are undone, but we are ourselves to blame. The little we gave has cost us all: had we not sacrificed the rights of the ash, we might ourselves have stood for ages." William Gilpin (see p. 54), the leading exponent of the picturesque in landscape, observed in his *Remarks on Forest Scenery* (1791), 'Wherever trees can be turned to profit they are commonly cut down, long before they attain picturesque commitment', while Sir John Sinclair, first President of the British Board of Agriculture, made the following rallying cry in 1803: 'Let us not be satisfied with the liberation of Egypt, or the subjugation of Malta, but let us subdue Finchley Common; let us conquer Hounslow Heath, let us compel Epping Forest to submit to the yoke of improvement.'[2]

(see p. 54)

Wenceslas Hollar (1607–77), *The woodman*, from John Ogilby, *Aesop's Fables and Aesopicks*, 1673. Etching, 16 x 10 cm.

Shrinkage of forest land due to enclosure and the transfer of common land to individual ownership were among targets of William Cobbett's criticism in *Rural Rides* (1822–6). In addition he inveighed against planting the wrong trees, also the subject of one of the last articles by Wangari Maathai (1940–2011), the Kenyan founder of the Green Belt Movement in East Africa and winner of the Nobel Peace Prize in 2004. In 2011, the International Year of Forests, Maathai highlighted the damage caused by introducing imported exotic species at the expense of indigenous ones:

> One of the most important environmental benefits indigenous forests provide is regulating climate and rainfall patterns; through harvesting and retaining rain, these forests release water slowly to springs, streams, and rivers; this reduces the speed of the water runoff and with it, soil erosion. Indigenous forests and trees also play an important role in spiritual and cultural life.
>
> Exotic trees, like pine and eucalyptus, cannot offer these environmental benefits. They eliminate most other plants and animals. Like invasive species, they create 'silent forests' that are devoid of wildlife, undergrowth and water.[3]

Forest or land spirit, made of wood. Melanau people, late 19th–early 20th century. H. 40 cm.

The figure was collected in Borneo (Sarawak) along the Igan River inhabited by the Melanau, for whom the tropical forest was the basis of their livelihood.

180

Dinabandhu Mahapatra, Trees of Orissa.
1982. Painting on tussar silk, 236 x 118 cm.

The trees allude to the story of the amorous
relationship between Krishna and Radha in
the twelfth-century poem the Gitagovinda.
They are copied from manuscripts in the
State Library in the eastern Indian state
of Orissa, now renamed Odisha, whose
extensive forest cover is at risk from mining
and related industrial activity.

Charles Wiener (1832–88), Bronze medal to commemorate the dedication of Epping Forest. 1882. Diam. 7.6 cm.

On the obverse is the bust of Queen Victoria, and on the reverse the inscription 'EPPING FOREST 6 MAY 1882 IT GIVES ME THE GREATEST SATISFACTION TO DEDICATE THIS BEAUTIFUL FOREST FOR THE USE AND ENJOYMENT OF MY PEOPLE FOR ALL TIME.'

Environmental damage is unceasing, and the scale of the problem has only grown exponentially; to take but one example, the vital biodiversity 'hotspot' of Madagascar (see p. 9) has lost eighty per cent of its forest cover in the past seventy-five years. Yet awareness of the perils of such action or neglect has never been absent. Good husbandry of natural resources is at the heart of the classical sources quoted in this book, while an understanding that the public good is inseparable from conservation and responsible management of the environment prompted legislation from the late nineteenth century onwards. The Epping Forest Act in 1878 saved the area from further enclosure; it was followed four years later by Queen Victoria's 'gift' of the forest to her subjects, which earned it the name 'The People's Forest'. The important psychological and cultural relationship between different communities and the forest, of which Wangari Maathai wrote, has been recognized by the protection of the dense forest of the Osun Sacred Grove on the outskirts of the city of Osogbo in Nigeria. Regarded as the abode of the goddess of fertility from the pantheon of Yoruba gods, it is one of the last remnants of primary high forest in southern Nigeria and the focus for an annual festival. UNESCO has inscribed forest sites around the world, including the Forest of the Cedars of God in northern Lebanon, where protection began in 1876 with the building of a high stone wall, paid for by Queen Victoria because of the trees' biblical significance. Now environmentalists realize that it is not enough to create conservation enclaves, national parks and World Heritage sites, but that land use strategies also must be developed for the areas surrounding them.

Botanic gardens or 'tree museums' are not mausoleums but living collections dedicated to preserving and cultivating species, often for propagation worldwide. Kew's Millennium Seedbank and its network of 120 partners in fifty-four countries has already collected and banked seeds from more than ten per cent of the world's wild plants, prioritizing those most threatened by extinction. One of the most remarkable discoveries of our lifetime has been *Wollemia nobilis*, or the Wollemi pine. The new species belongs to a genus previously known only from the fossil record of more than 65 million years ago. This was as exciting a revelation as the scene Jules Verne had imagined 130 years before in *Journey to the Centre of the Earth* (see p. 24). The genus *Wollemia* is related to that of *Agathis* (which includes the New

Wollemia nobilis (Wollemi pine), in the Australia Landscape at the British Museum, 2011, the fourth in a series of different habitats created by the Royal Botanic Gardens Kew in partnership with the British Museum.

Zealand Kauri tree) and *Araucaria* (that of the monkey puzzle tree), all three genera being placed in the family *Araucariaceae*. Since 2006 a propagation programme has made *Wollemia nobilis* available to botanic gardens first in Australia and then in other parts of the world, where it has proved its ability to thrive in very different environments, including the forecourt of the British Museum during the summer of 2011.

From 2008 to 2012 the British Museum, in partnership with the Royal Botanic Gardens Kew, has presented a series of landscapes in front of the Museum. The programme has celebrated the commitment of both institutions to strengthen cultural understanding, support biodiversity conservation across the world and raise awareness of the threat to fragile ecosystems on which everything – animal, vegetable or mineral – depends. These landscapes, covering China, India, South Africa, Australia and North America, have been described by visitors as providing 'tranquillity in the chaos' of the modern city. They are one testimonial to the importance the British Museum and Kew attach to continuing to lay 'bets on the human race', in the words of W.H. Auden, quoted at the very beginning of this book. If the fearsome prophecy in the Book of Isaiah (10:19) that 'the rest of the trees of his forest shall be few, that a child may write them' is not to be fulfilled, then we should take note of Antoine de Saint-Exupéry in *Wind, Sand and Stars* (1939). In this memoir, the French writer described how the Tuareg nomads from the Sahara, who accompanied him to Senegal, wept at their first sight of trees that hitherto they had known only from the Qur'an. Trees do indeed reveal a lot about a person, a society or a country's soul.

The China Landscape at the British Museum, 2008.

NOTES

INTRODUCTION

1. Pliny, *Natural History*, XII.1.2–11, p. 5. H. Rackham (transl.), *Pliny, Natural History. Volume IV: Books XII–XVI*, Cambridge MA and London 1968.
2. W. H. Auden, *Bucolics, II: Woods* (for Nicolas Nabokov), in Edward Mendelson (ed.), *Selected Poems*, Boston and London 1979, p. 206. Copyright © 1955 by W. H. Auden, renewed. Reprinted by permission of Curtis Brown, Ltd.
3. Virgil, *The Aeneid*, VI.154–5. W. F. Jackson Knight (transl.), *The Aeneid*, London, repr. 1966, pp. 151–2.
4. *Ibid.*, VIII.294–326, p. 210.
5. These were published by Sloane in his *Catalogus Plantarum Quae In Insula Jamaica*, London 1696, and in his illustrated two-volume *Voyage to the Islands Madera, Barbados, Nieves, S. Christophers, and Jamaica, with the Natural History of the Herbs and Trees, Four-footed Beasts, Fishes, Birds, Reptiles, &c.*, London 1707 and 1725. Sloane's herbarium is one of the core collections of the Natural History Museum, London.
6. *Captain Cook's Journal during His First Voyage Round the World in H.M. Bark Endeavour 1768–71*, a literal transcription of the original MSS edited by Captain W. J. L. Wharton, London 1893. Available online through Project Gutenberg, 2004: http://www.gutenberg.org/files/8106/8106-h/8106-h.html.
7. Erasmus Darwin, *The Loves of the Plants*, Canto II, London 1789, p. 155.
8. Charles Darwin, *The Origin of Species By Means Of Natural Selection*, J. W. Burrow (ed.), repr. London 1985, p. 172.

CHAPTER ONE

1. *See*, for example, Sandra Knapp's history of taxonomy on the Natural History Museum's website: http://www.nhm.ac.uk/nature-online/science-of-natural-history/taxonomy-systematics.
2. *Romeo and Juliet*, 2.1.85–6. Stanley Wells and Gary Taylor (eds), *The Oxford Shakespeare. The Complete Works*, Oxford 1995.
3. Pliny, *Natural History*, XXV.IV.8. W. H. S. Jones (transl.), *Pliny, Natural History, Volume VII: Books XXIV–XXVII*, Cambridge MA and London 1968, p. 141.
4. Robert Huxley, 'Challenging the dogma: classifying and describing the natural world', in Kim Sloan (ed.), *Enlightenment. Discovering the World in the Eighteenth Century*, London 2003, p. 73.
5. Nehemiah Grew, *The Anatomy of Plants with an Idea of a Philosophical History of Plants and several other Lectures read before the Royal Society*, London 1682, p. 6.
6. *Ibid.*, p. 9.

7. *Catalogus Plantarum Quae In Insula Jamaica*, London 1696.
8. Arthur MacGregor (ed.), *Sir Hans Sloane, Collector, Scientist, Antiquary*, London 1994, p. 15.
9. 'American Pine, long leaves repeating in groups of three; multiple cones arising together'.
10. *See* Barry Cunliffe, *Europe Between the Oceans. Themes and Variations: 9000 BC – AD 1000*, New Haven and London 2008, p. 89.
11. Alexander von Humboldt and Aimé Bonpland, *Essay on the Geography of Plants*, Stephen T. Jackson (ed. and intr.), Sylvie Romanowski (transl.), Chicago and London 2009, pp. 70–71. © 2009 by The University of Chicago.
12. Henry D. Thoreau, *Walden*, Jeffrey S. Cramer (ed.), Denis Donoghue (intr.), New Haven and London 2006, p. 89.
13. John Evelyn, *Sylva, or A Discourse of Forest Trees and the Propagation of Timber in his Majesties Dominions*, London 1664, Preface and pp. 1–2.
14. Anne Feuchter-Schawelka, Winfried Freitag and Dietger Grosser (eds), *Die Ebersberger Holzbibliothek: Vorgänger, Vorbilder und Nachfolger*, Ebersberg 2001, p. 31.
15. Diana Donald and Jane Munro (eds), *Endless Forms. Charles Darwin, Natural Science and the Visual Arts*, New Haven and London 2009, p. 8.
16. Jules Verne, *A Journey to the Centre of the Earth*, William Butcher (ed., transl. and notes), Oxford 1992, pp. 184–6. Reproduced by permission of Oxford University Press.
17. *See* J. R. Piggott, *Palace of the People. The Crystal Place at Sydenham 1854–1936*, London 2004, pp. 158–64.
18. *Ibid.*, p. 123.
19. Louis Figuier, *The World before the Deluge*, London 1865, p. 336.
20. *Ibid.*, pp. 141–2.
21. The fossil stumps visible today are internal casts formed by sand washed into the hollow centre of the decaying trunks and roots. This later hardened to sandstone with an outer layer of coal, formerly the tree bark, which was removed to reveal the sandstone casts.
22. Charles Darwin, *On the Origin of Species by Means of Natural Selection*, p. 171.
23. *See* Nathalie Gontier, 'Depicting the Tree of Life: the philosophical and historical roots of evolutionary tree diagrams', in *Evolution*, Education Outreach no. 4, 2011, pp. 515–38, and Theodore W. Pietsch, *Trees of Life. A Visual History of Evolution*, Baltimore 2012.

CHAPTER TWO

1. Robert Pogue Harrison, *Forests. The Shadow of Civilization*, Chicago and London 1997, pp. 7–8.
2. Mircea Eliade, *Patterns in Comparative Religion*, London 1958, 1979 (4th imp.), p. 286.
3. *See* Dominique Collon, *Ancient Near Eastern Art*, London 1995, p. 96.
4. From the 'standard inscription' carved across the centre of the wall panels from the Northwest Palace.
5. Colin McEwan and Leonardo Lopez Luján (eds), *Moctezuma. Aztec Ruler*, London 2009, cat. no. 90, pp. 206–7. *See also* Colin McEwan, Andrew Middleton et al, *Turquoise Mosaics from Mexico*, London 2006.
6. Wu Cheng'en, *Journey to the West (Hsi Yu Ki)*, W. J. F. Jenner (transl.), Beijing 2004 (4th printing), 6, p. 442. Another very good translation is by Anthony Yu, *The Journey to the West*, Chicago and London 1977, 2 vols.
7. *Ibid.*, pp. 489–90.
8. Anthony Storr (selected and intr.), *The Essential Jung. Selected Writings*, London 1998, p. 78.
9. Authorized version of the Bible, Genesis 2:8–9 and 15–17.
10. *Ibid.*, Revelation 22:1–2.
11. *See* Paul Binski, 'The Tree of Life', in *Becket's Crown. Art and Imagination in Gothic England 1170–1300*, New Haven and London 2004, pp. 209–29.
12. Mary Carruthers, 'Moving images in the mind's eye', in Jeffrey Hamburger and Anne-Marie Bouché (eds), *The Mind's Eye. Art and Theological Argument in the Middle Ages*, Princeton 2006, p. 288.
13. *See* David Bindman, 'The English Apocalypse', in Frances Carey (ed.), *The Apocalypse and the Shape of Things To Come*, London 1999, pp. 208–63.
14. *See* 'Archive for Research in Archetypal Symbols', *The Book of Symbols*, Cologne 2010.
15. Authorized version of the Bible, Isaiah 11:1.
16. Don Paterson, *Orpheus: A version of Rilke's 'Die Sonnette an Orpheus'*, London 2006, p. 3.
17. Dante, *The Divine Comedy*, Vol. 1: *The Inferno*. Mark Musa (transl.), London 1984, Canto I.3, p. 67. Courtesy of Indiana University Press.
18. *Ibid.*, Canto XIII.6, p. 186.
19. *See* Antony Griffiths, 'Callot: Miseries of War', in *Disasters of War: Callot, Goya, Dix*, National Touring Exhibition organized by the Hayward Gallery with the Department of Prints and Drawings, British Museum, London 1998, pp. 11–25.
20. *See* Philip Attwood and Felicity Powell, *Medals of Dishonour*, London 2009, cat. no. 19, p. 77.

21. Juliet Wilson-Bareau, 'Goya: the disasters of war', in *Disasters of War*, California 1999, pp. 28–55.

22. David Jones, *In Parenthesis*, London 1978, p. 184.

23. Frances Carey and Antony Griffiths, *Avant-garde British Printmaking 1914–1960*, London 1990, pp. 62–5.

24. *See* Thomas G. Ebrey, 'Printing to perfection: the colour-picture album', in Clarissa von Spee (ed.), *The Printed Image in China from the 8th to the 21st Centuries*, London 2010, pp. 26–35.

25. J. H. Fuseli, *Lectures on Painting*, London 1820, p. 179.

26. W. S. Gilpin, *Three essays on Picturesque Beauty*, London 1794 (2nd edn), pp. 100–101.

27. *Ibid.*, pp. 49–50.

28. Uvedale Price, *An Essay on the Picturesque as compared with the Sublime and the Beautiful*, London 1794, p. 76.

29. *Ibid.*, p. 190.

30. *See* William Vaughan, 'The primitive vision (1823–5)', in William Vaughan, Elizabeth Barker and Colin Harrison, *Samuel Palmer 1805–1881. Vision and Landscape*, London 2005, pp. 75–104.

31. John Ruskin, *Praeterita*, first published London 1885–9, 2nd edn 1907, Vol II, p. 113.

32. *Ibid.*, p. 112.

33. John Ruskin, *The Elements of Drawing*, London 1892, p. 169.

34. *See* Kim Sloan, *J. M. W. Turner. Watercolours from the R. W. Lloyd Bequest*, London 1998, no. 44, p. 126.

35. James George Frazer, *The Golden Bough*, Robert Fraser (ed., intr. and notes), Oxford 1994, pp. 806–7.

ADANSONIA

1. Rudyard Kipling, *The Elephant's Child*, in *Just So Stories* (1902), Jonathan Stroud (intr.), London 2008.

BETULA

1. John Evelyn, *Sylva*, pp. 141–2.

2. Robert Frost, *Birches* (1915), in Steven Croft (ed.), *Robert Frost. Selected Poems*, Oxford 2011, p. 45.

BROUSSONETIA PAPYRIFERA

1. Engelbert Kaempfer, *The history of Japan*, John Gaspar Scheuchzer (transl.), London 1727, p. 64.

2. Tsien Tsuen-Hsuin, *Paper and Printing*, Vol. V.1, Cambridge 1985, in Joseph Needham (ed.), *Science and Civilization in China*, 7 vols, Cambridge 1954–1999, pp. 57–9

BUXUS

1. *See* P. Kevin, James Robinson et al, 'A musical instrument fit for a queen: the metamorphosis of a medieval citole' in British Museum Technical Research Bulletin (2008), 2, pp. 13–27 and Jan Ellen Harriman, 'From gittern to citole' in *Early Music* (2011), 39 (1), pp. 139–40

2. William Vaughan, 'The primitive vision (1823–5)', in William Vaughan, Elizabeth Barker and Colin Harrison, *Samuel Palmer 1805–1881. Vision and Landscape*, London 2005, p. 98.

CEDRUS

1. *The Epic of Gilgamesh*, Tablet II.v.216, Andrew George (transl.), London 2003 (repr.), p. 19.

2. *Ibid.*, Tablet V.v 1, p. 39 and V. ISH 35' and 39', p. 46.

3. John Evelyn, *Sylva*, p. 59.

4. *The Epic of Gilgamesh*, Tablet V.v.295, p. 46.

5. *See* J. E. Curtis, *The Balawat Gates of Ashurnasirpal*, London 2008.

6. *Cymbeline*, 5.6.455–60. *The Oxford Shakespeare*.

COCOS NUCIFERA

1. *Narrative of the circumnavigation of the globe by the Austrian frigate Novara . . . 1857, 1858, & 1859*, London 1861–3.

2. Robert Louis Stevenson, *The Complete Works* Vol. 21, Newcastle upon Tyne 2009, pp. 43–47.

CRATAEGUS

1. *The History of that Holy Disciple Joseph of Arimathea*, 1770.

2. Richard Rawlinson, *The History and Antiquities of Glastonbury*, Oxford 1722, p. 222

3. www.everypoet.com/archive/poetry/Geoffrey_Chaucer/chaucer_poems_THE_COURT_OF_LOVE.htm

CUPRESSUS

1. *The Metamorphoses of Ovid,* Mary M. Innes (transl.), Harmondsworth, 1955, repr. 1970 , X.105–8, pp. 227–8 and 137–42, p. 228

2. Pliny, *Natural History*, XVI.LIX.139, p. 479.

3. Henry D. Thoreau, *Walden*, Jeffrey S. Cramer (ed.), Denis Donoghue (intr.), New Haven and London 2006, for the quotation Thoreau gives from Gulistan. The ref. is p. 84.

FICUS

1. James Fenton (ed.), *D. H. Lawrence. Selected Poems*, London 2008, p. 93.

2. John Evelyn, *Sylva*.

3. Pliny, *Natural History*, XV.XXI.82, p. 345.

4. Mas'ūdī, *The Meadows of Gold*, Penguin Great Journeys, London 2007, p. 47.

FRAXINUS

1. John Evelyn, p. 23.

2. Homer, *The Iliad*, Robert Fagles (transl.), London 1991, 19.459–63, p. 501

3. Roger Deakin, *Wildwood: a Journey through Trees*, London 2006, pp. 382–3.

GINKGO BILOBA

1. Engelbert Kaempfer, *The history of Japan*, John Gaspar Scheuchzer (transl.), London 1727, p. 66.

2. From Goethe's *West-östlicher Diwan* (1819), in *Goethe. Selected Verse*, David Luke (transl. and ed.), London 1986, p. 249. © David Luke, 1964.

LAURUS NOBILIS

1. *The Metamorphoses of Ovid*, I.518–557, p. 43

2. Pliny, *Natural History*, XV.XL.136–7, p. 381.

MALUS

1. Homer, *The Odyssey*, Robert Fagles (transl.), London 1997, 24.379–380, p. 479

2. *The Metamorphoses of Ovid*, XIV.623–633, p. 328

3. Hesiod, *The Theogeny*, 285–287, C. A. Elton (transl.), London and New York n.d. (one of Sir John Lubbock's Hundred Books published by Routledge from 1896).

MORUS

1. Pliny, *Natural History,* XV.XXVII.97, p. 355.

OLEA

1. Homer, *The Odyssey*, 13.108–117, p. 289

2. Pliny, *Natural History*, XV.III.11–12, p. 295.

3. *Ibid.*, XV.v.19, p. 301.

PINUS

1. Virgil, *The Aeneid*, IX.83–93, p. 227

2. *Three Hundred Tang Poems*, Peter Harris (transl.), London 2009, pp. 225–6.

POPULUS

1. 'The Interpreter's House', no. 28, February 2005, p. 41.

PRUNUS

1. *The Poems of Mao Zedong*, Willis Barnstone (transl, intr. and notes) Berkeley, Los Angeles and London 2008, p. 105.

2. Pliny, *Natural History,* XV.XII.45, p. 319.

3. The Oxford Shakespeare. 2.2 238–243, p. 1235

4. Engelbert Kaempfer, *The history of Japan*, John Gaspar Scheuchzer (transl.), London 1727, p. 66.

5. Pliny, *Natural History*, XV. xxx.102–3, p. 359.

QUERCUS

1. Herodotus, *The Histories*. Robin Waterfield (transl.), Oxford 1998, 2.54–55, p. 117.

2. Homer, *The Odyssey*, 14.370–3, p. 312

3. Pliny, *Natural History*, XVI.II.6–7, p. 391 and V.II, p. 395.

4. Pliny, *Natural History*, XVI.VI.15, p.397.

5. Quoted in Antony Griffiths and Frances Carey, *German Printmaking in the Age of Goethe*, London 1994, p. 114.

6. *See* Charlotte Gere and Judy Rudoe, *Jewellery in the Age of Queen Victoria. A Mirror to the Age*, London 2010, pp. 105–6

7. Pliny, *Natural History*, XVI.XCV.249, p. 549.

8. *See* Barry Cunliffe, *Druids. A Very Short Introduction*, Oxford 2010.

ZIZIPHUS

1. Pliny, *Natural History*, XIII.XIII.111, p. 165.

2. *See* John Cherry, *The Holy Thorn Reliquary*, London 2010.

EPILOGUE

1. *Big Yellow Taxi*. Words and music by Joni Mitchell. © 1970 (Renewed), Crazy Crow Music. All rights administered by Sony/ATV Music Publishing, 8 Music Square West, Nashville, TN 37203. All Rights Reserved.

2. Revd John Sinclair, *Life and Works of The Late Right Honourable Sir John Sinclair*, 2 vols, Edinburgh 1837, I, p. 111.

3. Wangari Maathai, 'The silent forests', in *The Guardian*, 25 November 2011.

FURTHER READING

Terese Tse Bartholomew, *Hidden Meanings in Chinese Art*, San Francisco 2006

Maggie Campbell-Culver, *A Passion for Trees. The Legacy of John Evelyn*, London 2006

Charles Darwin, *The Origin of Species by Means of Natural Selection*, London 1985

Diana Donald and Jane Munro (eds), *Endless Forms. Charles Darwin, Natural Science and the Visual Arts*, New Haven and London 2009

Mircea Eliade, *Patterns in Comparative Religion*, London 1958, 4th imp. 1979

John Evelyn, *Sylva or a Discourse of Forest Trees and the Propagation of Timber in His Majesty's Dominions*, London 1664 (http://openlibrary.org/books/OL13518723M/Sylva)

James George Frazer, *The Golden Bough*. Edited with an introduction and notes by Robert Fraser, Oxford, 1994

Fred Hageneder, *The Living Wisdom of Trees*, London 2005

Robert Pogue Harrison, *Forests. The Shadow of Civilization*, Chicago and London 1997

Charlie Jarvis, *Order out of Chaos*, London 2007

Tony Kirkham, *Wilson's China: A Century On*, Kew 2009

Mark Laird and Alicia Weisberg-Roberts (eds), *Mrs Delany and Her Circle*, New Haven and London 2009

William Bryant Logan, *Oak. The Frame of Civilization*, New York 2006

Neil MacGregor, *A History of the World in 100 Objects*, London 2010

Joseph Needham, *Science and Civilization in China: vol. 6, part 1, Botany*, Cambridge 1986

Therese O'Malley and Amy W. Meyers (eds), *The Art of Natural History: Illustrated Treatises and Botanical Paintings 1400-1850*, New Haven and London, 2008

The Metamorphoses of Ovid, Mary M. Innes (transl), Harmondsworth 1955, repr. 1970

Thomas Pakenham, *Remarkable Trees of the World*, London 2002

Anna Pavord, *The Naming of Names*, London 2005

Theodore W. Pietsch, *Trees of Life. A Visual History of Evolution*, Baltimore 2012

Pliny the Elder, *Natural History*, 10 vols, Cambridge 1910–62

Oliver Rackham, *Ancient Woodland: Its History, Vegetation and Uses in England*, London 1980

Jonathan Roberts, *Mythic Woods. The World's Most Remarkable Forests*, London 2004

Simon Schama, *Landscape and Memory*, London 1995

Kim Sloan, *'A noble art'* in *Amateur Artists and Drawing Masters c.1600-1800*, London 2000

Kim Sloan (ed.) *Enlightenment. Discovering the World in the Eighteenth Century*, London 2003. (In particular the section on the Natural World with chapters by Robert Huxley and Jill Cook.)

Henry D. Thoreau, *Walden* Jeffrey S. Cramer (ed.), New Haven and London 2006

Colin Tudge, *The Secret Life of Trees. How They Live and Why They Matter*, London 2005

Virgil, *Georgics* in *Eclogues, Georgics, Aeneid, 1–6*, H. R. Fairclough (transl.), Cambridge and London 1986

Alexandra Walsham, *The Reformation of the Landscape. Religion, Identity, and Memory on Early Modern Britain and Ireland*, Oxford 2011

Andrea Wulf, *The Brother Gardeners*, London 2008

WEB RESOURCES

The British Museum collection online: To find out more about objects in all areas of the British Museum, visit britishmuseum.org/research/search_the_collection_database.aspx

Royal Botanic Gardens, Kew: http://www.kew.org

Natural History Museum, London: http://www.nhm.ac.uk/research-curation/departments/botany/index.html

The Plant List: http://www.theplantlist.org/
Started in 2010 as a joint project between the Royal Botanic Gardens, Kew and Missouri Botanical Garden, this provides a working list of all known plant species.

ACKNOWLEDGEMENTS

The author wishes to thank the following connected with British Museum Press for the production of this book, in particular Felicity Maunder on the editorial side, with assistance from Carolyn Jones; Axelle Russo for sourcing the pictures, Raymonde Watkins for the design, and Charlotte Cade and Emma Poulter for seeing it through to final publication.

Abundant thanks are due to the many people who have contributed and checked information:

Philip Attwood
Giulia Bartrum
Lissant Bolton
Caroline Cartwright
Hugo Chapman
Jill Cook
John Curtis
Catherine Eagleton
Kazayuki Enami
Philippa Edwards
Irving Finkel
Celina Fox
Kathryn Godwin
Amanda Gregory
Alfred Haft

Jill Hasell
Thomas Hockenhull
Alison Hollis
Charlie Jarvis
Jonathan King
Tony Kirkham
Anouska Komlosy
Ian Jenkins
Mark McDonald
Richard Parkinson
Venetia Porter
Sascha Priewe
Judy Rudoe
Kim Sloan
Chris Spring

Jan Stuart
Dora Thornton
Hiromi Uchida
Helen Wang
Frances Wood

PICTURE CREDITS

PAGE
1 P&E M.6903
2 PD 1943,0410.1
6, 8 (top) Asia 1993,0724,0.2 (Funded by the Brooke Sewell Permanent Fund)
8 (bottom) AOA Af1939,34.1 (Acquired with the assistance of the Art Fund)
9 (top) © The Natural History Museum, London
9 (bottom) P&E 1986,1201.1–27 (Donated by the Somerset Levels Project and Fisons PLC)
10 © The Natural History Museum, London
11 PD 1897,0505.895 (Bequeathed by Augusta Hall, Baroness Llanover)
12 PD 1985,1214.8
17 PD 1923,1112.174
18 (top) P&E 2010,8035.1 (Donated by A.W. Milburn)
18 (bottom) ME 1896,0406.7
19 PD 1848,1013.138

20 (top) PD 1909,0512.1(12)
20 (bottom) PD 2009,7037.9 (Donated by and © Lyn Williams)
21 PD 1977,0507.3
23 PD 1985,1214.8
24 PD 1901,1105.53 (Donated by F.W. Baxter)
25 © The British Library Board
26 © The British Library Board
27 © The British Library Board
28 PD 1935,0522.3.51
31 ME 1849,0502.15
32 (top) P&E Eu,SLMisc.1103 (Bequeathed by Sir Hans Sloane)
32 (bottom) AOA Am,St.397.a
33 Asia 1956,0714,0.5
34 Asia As1859,1228.493 (Donated by Revd William Charles Raffles Flint)
35 ME As1997,24.12 (Donated by Ken Ward)
36 (left) PD 1935,0522.3.52
36 (right) PD 1935,0522.3.53
37 PD 1935,0522.3.51
38 PD 1847,0318.93.76
39 PD 1851,0901.921 (Donated by William Smith)
40 PD 1864,0813.291
41 © source, ARTFL University of Chicago
42 (left) Asia 1875,0617.1
42 (right) PD 1904,0723.1

43 PD 1871,0812.811
44 PD 1892,0411.6 (Donated by Charles Fairfax Murray)
45 PD 1983,1001.7
46 AOA Af2006,15.40
47 AOA Am1990,08.167
48 AOA Af2005,01.1; reproduced by permission of the artists
50 PD 1918,0413.5 (Purchase funded by Sir Ernest Ridley Debenham, 1st Baronet)
51 (top) PD 1861,0713.787
51 (bottom left) CM 1978,1206.1
51 (bottom right) PD 1975,1025.251
52 PD 1918,0219.10 (Donated by Christopher Richard Wynne Nevinson)
53 PD 1918,0704.8 (Donated by Ernest Brown & Phillips)
54 Asia 1928,0301,0.1 (Donated by K.K. Chow)
55 (top) PD Gg,3.365 (Bequeathed by Clayton Mordaunt Cracherode)
55 (bottom) PD 1973,U.967 (Bequeathed by Clayton Mordaunt Cracherode)
56 PD 1864,1114.216
57 PD 1964,1104.1.3
58 PD 1987,0725.17
59 PD 1958,0712.444 (Bequeathed by Robert Wylie Lloyd)
60 PD 1989,0930.138

62 (top) CM 1984,0605.888; reproduced with the kind permission of the BCEAO
62 (bottom) AOA Oc1939,12.3 (Donated by A.G. Hemming)
63 AOA Af2002,09.21; © Seif Rashidi Kiwamba, Tinga Tinga studio
64 (top) P&E 1953,0208.14–15 (Donated by Sir Grahame Douglas Clark)
64 (left) GR 1983,1229.1
65 PD 2000,0520.4
66 (top) Am1949,22.170
66 (bottom left) AOA Am,SLMisc.2065.1–30 (Bequeathed by Sir Hans Sloane)
66 (bottom right) AOA Am2003,19.1, 20, 21a–b, 22 and 23 (Purchased through the Heritage Lottery Fund with contributions from the British Museum Friends, J.P. Morgan Chase and the Art Fund)
67 AOA Am1989,21.6
68 PD 1888,0215.68 (Donated by Isabel Constable)
69 PD 2003,0131.16 (Donated by James F. White); © Robert Kipniss
70 Asia 1963,0731,0.3
71 (left) Asia As,+.4033 (Donated by Thomas Watters)
71 (right) Asia As,+.4037 (Donated by Thomas Watters)

72 AOA Oc.4252

73 (*top*) AOA Oc,A37.1; © The Estate of Katesa Schlosser

73 (*bottom*) AOA Oc,G.N.1638 (Donated by Mrs J.J. Lister)

74, 75 P&E 1963,1002.1 (Purchased with contributions from the Pilgrim Trust and the Art Fund)

76 P&E WB.232 (Bequeathed by Baron Ferdinand Anselm de Rothschild)

77 (*top*) PD 1939,0114.7 (Donated by the Art Fund)

77 (*bottom*) PD 1919,0528.2

78 (*top*) ME 1881,1109.1

78 (*bottom*) ME 1848,1104.127

79 EA 35285

80 (*top*) PD 1950,1111.56 (Purchase funded by the H.L. Florence Fund)

80 (*bottom*) PD 1878,1228.135 (Bequeathed by John Henderson)

81 PD SL,5284.62 (Bequeathed by Sir Hans Sloane)

82 (*left*) AOA Oc.4790 (Donated by Henry Christy)

82 (*right*) PD 1890,0512.107

83 AOA Af1898,0115.173 (Donated by the Secretary of State for Foreign Affairs)

84 (*top*) AOA Oc,B13.9

84 (*bottom*) AOA Oc1931,0714.8 (Donated by Lady Elsie Elizabeth Allardyce)

85 (*top*) AOA As1887,1015.149 (Donated by Edward Horace Man)

85 (*bottom*) AOA Oc1993,03.60

86 PD 1897,0505.246 (Bequeathed by Augusta Hall, Baroness Llanover)

87 (*left*) P&E 1887,0307.1.23 (Donated by Augustus Wollaston Franks)

87 (*right*) PD 1856,0209.422

88 (*left*) PD 1874,0711.2095

88 (*right*) P&E 1978,1002.1060 (Prof. John Hull Grundy and Anne Hull Grundy)

89 (*left*) PD 1933,0411.119 (Donated through The Art Fund)

89 (*right*) PD 1955,0420.7 (Donated by H. Megarity)

90 (*left*) PD 1950,0520.444

90 (*right*) CM 2002,0102.4701 (Bequeathed by Charles A. Hersh)

91 ME 1974,0617,0.13.48v–49r

92 ME 1974,0617,0.3.26

93 ME G.308 (Donated by Frederick du Cane Godman and Miss Edith Godman)

94 PD 1962,0714.1.47

95 PD 1890,0512.133

96 (*left*) Photo courtesy of Richard Wilford, Kew; © The Trustees of the Royal Botanical Gardens, Kew

96 (*right*) PD 1871,0610.536

97 (*left*) AOA Oc1989,05.12; © DACS 2012

97 (*right*) PD 2002,0929.100 (Donated by Lyn Williams); © The Estate of Fred Williams

98 (*left*) EA 5396

98 (*right*) PD 1907,1001.14 (Donated by George Dunlop Leslie)

99 (*left*) P&E 1856,0623.5

99 (*right*) PD E,7.268

100 (*top*) PD 1897,0505.331 (Bequeathed by Augusta Hall, Baroness Llanover)

100 (*bottom*) EA 37983

101 (*left*) ME 1941,0712,0.5 (Purchase funded by the Art Fund)

101 (*right*) PD 1997,1109,0.4

102 (*left*) Asia 1919,0101,0.6

102 (*right*) PD 1996,0330,0.4 (Donated by Miss Ione Moncrieff St George Brett)

103 (*left*) AOA 2008,2021.2; © Sarah Kizza

103 (*right*) AOA Am2006,Drg.2896

104 (*top*) PD 1912,0819.6 (Donated by Henry Currie Marillier)

104 (*bottom*) P&E 1952,0202.2 (Donated by Major M.C. Donovan through Sir R.E. Mortimer Wheeler)

105 GR 1836,0224.127

106 (*top*) PD 2004,0601.49 (Bequeathed by Alexander Walker); © David Nash. All rights reserved, DACS 2012

106 (*right*) AOA Am2003,19.14 (Purchased with contributions from J.P. Morgan Chase, the British Museum Friends, the Art Fund and the Heritage Lottery Fund)

107 PD 1888,0215.67 (Donated by Isabel Constable)

108 (*left*) © The Trustees of the Royal Botanical Garden, Kew

108 (*top right*) P&E 1989,0105.1

108 (*bottom right*) Asia OA+.3163

109 Asia 2004,0330,0.4 (Donated by Kiyota Yûji); © Kiyota Yûji Work

110 AOA Am1949,22.118

111 (*left*) © Natural History Museum, London

111 (*right*) AOA Am1977,Q.3

112 P&E 1855,1201.103

113 PD H,2.27

114 GR 1857,1220.434

115 GR 1939,0607.1 (Purchased with contribution from the Art Fund)

115 (*right*) P&E M.6903

116 PD 1913,0714.69

117 (*left*) PD SL,5226.96 (Bequeathed by Sir Hans Sloane)

117 (*right*) P&E 1989,1103.1

118 GR 1805,0703.38

119 (*left*) PD E,2.7 (Bequeathed by Joseph Nollekens through Francis Douce)

119 (*right*) P&E 1958,1201.3268

120 PD 1962,0714.1.40

121 (*top*) PD 1887,0502.113 (Donated by Samuel Calvert)

121 (*bottom*) P&E 1923,0216.3.CR (Donated by James Powell & Sons, Whitefriars Glassworks)

122 PD 1938,1209.3 (Donated by E. Kersley)

123 PD 1929,1109.4 (Donated by Henry van den Bergh through the Art Fund)

124 (*top*) Asia 1938,0524.179

124 (*bottom*) Asia MAS.926.a–b

125 PD SL,5284.101 (Bequeathed by Sir Hans Sloane)

126 (*top*) Asia 1908,0718,0.2 (Donated by Sir Hickman Bacon)

126 (*bottom*) Asia 1907,1111.73

127 PD 1948,0410.4.214 (Bequeathed by Sir

Hans Sloane)

128 PD 1869,1009.30

129 P&E 1864,0816.1 (Bequeathed by George Daniel)

130 PD 1841,1211.59

131 GR 1837,0609.42

132 (*top*) ME OA+.4286

132 (*bottom*) GR 2001,0508.1 (Purchased with a contribution from the Olympic Museum)

133 (*top*) PD 1861,0713.430

133 (*bottom*) GR 1868,0105.46 (Donated by Dr George Witt)

134 P&E SLMisc.151 (Bequeathed by Sir Hans Sloane)

135 PD 1957,1214.148

136 (*left*) P&E WB.229 (Bequeathed by Baron Ferdinand Anselm de Rothschild)

136 (*right*) PD 1890,0415.412 (Donated by Miss Sarah Deacon)

137 PD SL,5218.167 (Bequeathed by Sir Hans Sloane)

138 (*top*) CM C.4884

138 (*bottom*) AOA Am1991,09.10.a–b

139 (*top*) Asia 1881,1210,0.1895

139 (*bottom*) Asia 1945,1017.418 (Bequeathed by Oscar Charles Raphael)

140 Asia 1973,0917,0.59.24

141 (*left*) GR 1856,1226.1007 (Bequeathed by Sir William Temple)

141 (*bottom*) PD 1974,0615.28 (Donated by Dame Joan Evans)

141 (*right*) PD 1974,1207.17 (Donated by Miss Rowlands)

142 PD SL,5284.111 (Bequeathed by Sir Hans Sloane)

143 PD 2003,0630.91 (Funded by Arcana Foundation)

144 PD 1895,0915.517

145 PD 1868,0808.9382

146 Asia 1910,0212,0.476

147 (*left*) Asia PDF.815 (On loan from Sir Percival David Foundation of Chinese Art)

147 (*right*) Asia 1914,0319,0.2

148 Asia 1948,0410,0.65 (Donated by Henry Bergen)

149 (*left*) PD 1897,0505.710 (Bequeathed by Augusta Hall, Baroness Llanover)

149 (*right*) Asia 1936,0413.8 (Bequeathed by Reginald Radcliffe Cory)

150 PD SL,5219.144 (Bequeathed by Sir Hans Sloane)

151 (*left*) PD 1962,0714.1.36

151 (*bottom*) Asia Franks.2455 (Donated by Sir Augustus Wollaston Franks)

151 (*right*) Asia 1936,0413.44 (Bequeathed by Reginald Radcliffe Cory)

152 (*top*) Asia 1992,0416,0.4.10 (Purchase funded by the Brooke Sewell Permanent Fund)

152 (*bottom*) P&E 1988,0705.1, 6, 7

153 (*left*) Asia 1906,1220,0.1778

153 (*right*) Asia 1982,0518.1

154 (*left*) GR 1908,0414.1

154 (*right*) P&E 1938,0202.1 (Purchased with contributions from the Art Fund and the Christy Fund)

155 PD 1943,0410.1

156 PD 1917,1208.250 (Donated by Nan Ino Cooper, Baroness Lucas of Crudwell and Lady Dingwall, in memory of Auberon Thomas Herbert, 9th Baron Lucas of Crudwell and 5th Lord Dingwall)

157 (*bottom*) P&E 1978,1002.312 (Donated by Professor John Hull Grundy and Anne Hull Grundy)

157 (*right*) PD 2008,7057.1; © ARS, NY and DACS, London 2012

158 (*left*) PD 1870,0709.283

158 (*right*) CM M.8596

159 (*left*) P&E 1944,1001.20 (Donated by Miss M.H. Turner)

159 (*right*) P&E 1935,0716.1.CR (Donated by Mrs Charles J. Lomax in memory of her husband)

160 PD 2001,0330.11 (Purchase funded by the British Museum Friends)

161 (*top*) PD 1878,0713.1275

161 (*bottom*) P&E 1863,1207.1 (Donated by Queen Victoria)

162 PD 1868,0808.6051

163 PD F,5.33 (Bequeathed by Clayton Mordaunt Cracherode)

164 (*left*) AOA Am1903,-63

164 (*right*) P&E Eu2005,0506.28

165 (*top*) P&E R.30 (Donated by Augustus Wollaston Franks)

165 (*bottom*) CM CIB.16027 (Donated by ifs School of Finance)

166 PD Y,5.62 (Donated by Dorothea Banks)

167 PD 1897,0505.851 (Bequeathed by Augusta Hall, Baroness Llanover)

168 (*top*) PD Banks,2*.6

168 (*bottom left*) AOA Am1981,Q.1921

168 (*bottom right*) AOA Am,NWC.43 (Donated by Sir Joseph Banks)

169 PD 1932,0213.14 (Donated by G.C. Allingham)

170 PD SL,5275.26 (Bequeathed by Sir Hans Sloane)

171 (*top*) House of Commons Library, on loan to the British Museum

171 (*bottom*) P&E 2005,0604.1–2

172 (*top*) PD D,2.2382 (Donated by Dorothea Banks)

172 (*bottom*) AOA Af2006,12.6; © Daniel Oblie

173 (*top*) PD 1979,0623.15.3

173 (*bottom*) AOA Am1989,12.126

174 Asia 1999,0203,0.8 (Bequeathed by Major J.P.S. Pearson)

175 PD 1921,0411.1; © Ed Ruscha

176 P&E WB.67 (Bequeathed by Baron Ferdinand Anselm de Rothschild)

177 (*left*) PD 1867,0309.1712

177 (*right*) PD SL,5284.111 (Bequeathed by Sir Hans Sloane)

178 CM 1986,0209.1; © Ronald Pennell

179 Asia 1842,1210.1

180 (left) Asia As1905,-.648

180 (right) PD 1854,0708.135

181 Asia 1989,0204,0.70; © Dinabandhu Mahapatra

182 (left) CM M.9137

182 (right) Photo: Richard Wilford

183 Photo: Richard Wilford

INDEX

Page numbers in *italics* refer to captions/illustrations